"A common-sense approach to combining the right amount of love and accountability to lift people and organizations to new heights."

—JON GORDON
Eleven-Time Best-Selling Author of
The Power of Positive Leadership and *The Energy Bus*

"When Dr. Peddy talks about 'lifting,' he is talking about caring, coaching, and having the courage necessary to help people be the best they can be. Anybody that has a team needs to read this book and learn how to 'lift' using the three C's!"

—DAMON WEST
Keynote Speaker and
Best-Selling Author of *The Coffee Bean*

Lift for Principals

LIFT

for

PRINCIPALS

*Growing Teachers
to Be Their Best Selves*

Dr. Walter Peddy

BROWN BOOKS
PUBLISHING GROUP

Lift for Principals
Growing Teachers to Be Their Best Selves

Brown Books Publishing Group
Dallas, TX / New York, NY
www.BrownBooks.com
(972) 381-0009

A New Era in Publishing®

Publisher's Cataloging-In-Publication Data

Names: Peddy, Walter, author.
Title: Lift for principals : growing teachers to be their best selves /
    Dr. Walter Peddy.
Description: Dallas, TX ; New York, NY : Brown Books Publishing
    Group, [2022] | Includes bibliographical references.
Identifiers: ISBN 9781612545424 (hardcover) | ISBN 9781612545431
    (ebook)
Subjects: LCSH: School principals. | Educational leadership. | Teachers.
Classification: LCC LB2831.9 .P43 2022 (print) | LCC LB2831.9 (ebook)
    | DDC 371.2012--dc23

ISBN 978-1-61254-542-4
LCCN 2021921568

Printed in the United States
10 9 8 7 6 5 4 3 2 1

For more information or to contact the author, please go to
www.LeadingIsLifting.com.

To Amanda, Landon, and Hayden.

Contents

Part III: COURAGE

Part IV: A WAY TO LIFT

Introduction

This book is for you, the school principal. You are the unsung hero, the person behind the scenes who holds the line against unruly parents, needy superintendents, and meddling board members so that teachers can teach and students can learn. I have always thought the author of the following Senate Committee Report, written over forty years ago, got it right:

> *In many ways the school principal is the most important and influential individual in any school. He or she is the person responsible for all the activities that occur in and around the school, the climate for teaching, the level of professionalism and morale of teachers, and the degree of concern for what students may or may not become. The principal is the main link between the community and the school, and the way he or she performs in this capacity largely determines the attitudes of parents and students about the school. If a school is a vibrant, innovative, child-centered place, if it has a reputation for excellence in teaching, if students are performing to the best of their ability, one can almost always point to the principal's leadership as the key to success.* (1977 US Senate Committee Report on Equal Educational Opportunity)

Next to the classroom teacher, the principal has the greatest impact on student achievement (Fullan 2009). For our children to get the most out of their school experience, our schools need our school principals to be their best.

And yet, how can they be? Layered in minutia, the job has changed dramatically in the fifteen years I have been an administrator. Education has become a catch-all answer for every societal ill imaginable. Social media disruptions, bad parenting, and the politicization of education have burdened school leadership with challenges beyond that of setting high standards for teaching and learning.

My appreciation for you—the principal—and my understanding of the importance and difficulty of your job inspired me to write this book. The best school leaders (or any leaders for that matter) understand that the quality of an organization depends on the quality of its employees. Great teachers (the number one reason students succeed) make great schools, and great principals know how to help teachers to be their best. That is what *Lift for Principals* is about.

Think about rocking chairs. Have you ever sat in one? Did you feel secure? Stable? Supported? If so, the rocking chair was made well. You may have wanted to sit in it forever. Good leaders, like good rocking chairs, firmly support others. But there's more to it.

For students to achieve, principals must be people-builders; they will not let teachers stay in that comfortable place, no matter how much teachers may want to. For teachers to be great, principals must move beyond support, which is really doing just enough to keep people from falling, and become lifting leaders. When principals lift, they do the three things necessary to elevate the performance of their teachers: they show that they care, they coach, and they display the courage to help their people achieve excellence. They lift.

In *Lift for Principals*, I focus on helping the following groups of leaders improve:

- New leaders that need a way to elevate the performance of their teachers.
- Veteran leaders who want to get better at the developmental supervision of teachers.
- Successful leaders who continually seek to better develop, coach, and mentor teachers.

When you finish this book, take a hard look at your priorities, your processes, and your performance and determine honestly whether you have earned the right to lift your teachers. If you have, great! You are ready to elevate the performance of others around you. If you haven't, you will know clearly the steps you must take. The journey from good to great, mediocrity to mastery, and average to excellent requires your commitment to lift as a leader.

Lift for Principals has two components. The first is the parable of Colby, a new high school principal who inherits a campus that is in danger of being shut down by the state. Parables convey moral truths or life lessons—Colby's story illustrates what it means to lift. Colby's parable is divided into three sections, each followed by a reflection. The important leadership principles of caring, coaching, and showing courage when necessary are the focal points of the reflections. You have to earn the right to lift as a leader, and these sections will help you determine whether you are ready.

The second component of this book is a model that marries the concepts of lifting leadership with the work of Carl Glickman, teacher and author of many books, including *Leadership For Learning: How to Help Teachers Succeed*. With this model, you will have a way to apply the lifting formula in your own work context. You will start elevating the performance of your teachers and evaluating both their improvement and your effectiveness as a lifting leader.

My greatest hope for you is that after reading this book, you will "do school" differently. I hope you will no longer let the madness and minutia of the job derail you from making the impact your teachers and students deserve. I hope you will step back and make a decision to budget your time differently. By focusing each day on caring, coaching, and acting with courage, you can and will become the school leader you were born to be.

PART
I

CARING

Chapter 1

The Honeymoon

Colby Owen felt the adrenaline course throughout his body as the reality began to sink in. He would be the next high school principal at Kinney High School!

"Yes ma'am," he told Dr. Yates, the school superintendent. "I am incredibly excited and ready for the opportunity. I will not let you down."

At thirty-one years old, Colby recognized the incredible trust Dr. Yates was putting in him to lead Kinney. The staff consisted primarily of veteran teachers who might have reservations about such a young leader taking the reins at a campus that had some serious academic concerns.

Not many people had applied for the job, but that fact did little to dampen Colby's enthusiasm for his new role. He had faced adversity before, and viewed obstacles as opportunities. As an outsider new to the district, he had some time to get acclimated; a two-year contract allowed him to honeymoon for a little while. Dr. Yates wanted results though. She had made that abundantly clear during the interview process.

Colby considered the challenges facing him at Kinney, learned through the interview process and his own research of the campus. Low student attendance, poor teacher morale, and sub-par academic data all pointed to a once proud high school in the early stages of decline. The state had labeled the school as "low performing." A few more years of poor results would result in a state takeover of the district. The consequences of a state takeover were many. Reduced funding, teacher layoffs, and the replacement of the school board and current administrative personnel were certain if Kinney High School didn't get back on track.

Colby smiled as he remembered one of Grandpa Wright's favorite sayings. As a boy, Colby sometimes faced tasks he thought too big for him, such as push-mowing his neighbor's three-acre yard or feeding and watering Grandpa Wright's livestock in the hour of dawn before school. When Colby insisted that these tasks were impossible, Grandpa Wright invariably said, "Colby, how do you eat an elephant?"

As Colby pondered the gargantuan task of righting the ship at Kinney, he answered no one in particular: "One bite at a time."

When Colby was two, his parents took a flight from which they never returned. His parents' last will and testament dictated a unique arrangement. Until he was ready for life on his own, Colby would split his time between the homes of his two grandfathers. Grandpa Wright, his mother's father, owned a construction company and lived on a small farm on the east side of town. Grandpa Owen lived on the west side in a neat two-story home in the town's only subdivision. He owned and managed the town's only supermarket, at which he had worked since the age of fourteen.

As peculiar as the arrangement was to the outside world, to Colby it was just right. Both homes were loving, safe, and fun in distinct ways.

The opportunity to help both Grandpa Wright with chores around the farm and Grandpa Owen with some of the smaller tasks around his home ensured Colby was rarely bored. As he got older, he spent a great deal of time working for Grandpa Wright on various construction projects during the summer and assisting on weekends at Grandpa Owen's grocery store. As different as these two men were, they were similar in many ways. One of their strongest similarities was their penchant for hard work.

Grandpa Wright was big, strong, and imposing to anyone who didn't know him. His hands were the size of cinder blocks; anyone brave enough to shake his right hand often heard and felt the popping of bones from the pressure. Grandpa Wright had a deep voice, wide shoulders, and a large belly that suggested years of devouring as much bacon and eggs as he could shove onto a breakfast plate. His signature outfit included brown steel-toed boots, denim overalls, and V-necked T-shirts; it wasn't until those shirts turned to a rusty color that Grandma Gloria could convince him to go buy a new set.

Grandpa Wright was a World War II veteran who met General MacArthur during his service in the South Pacific.

Colby spent hours listening to Grandpa Wright tell stories about his time as a soldier. He heard many of those stories during lunch breaks with Grandpa Wright's numerous construction crews. More often than not, Grandpa Wright's old Dodge truck pulled up on the job site just as the men were breaking for lunch. He walked up to whatever shaded tree the crew sat under and regaled the men with one of the dozens of stories from his time in the Great War.

Quick to anger and to laugh, Grandpa Wright was a stark contrast to Grandpa Owen. Thin and reserved, Grandpa Owen selected his words carefully for effect. If Grandpa Owen had something to say, people leaned in and listened hard; it was usually significant.

"Every word you say has weight," Grandpa Owen repeated often to Colby. Colby had a great deal of energy, and after a week of listening to tales at Grandpa Wright's house, he often couldn't wait to retell some of them. Though patient beyond measure, even Grandpa Owen eventually set his gaze on Colby and reminded him that most people can't think and talk at the same time. This was an effective way of redirecting Colby to more productive avenues.

While not as boisterous as Grandpa Wright, Grandpa Owen was respected and liked. Like Grandpa Wright, he was an early riser and fully engaged wherever he was, be it the grocery store, home, or church. Grandpa Owen was a man of focus, and he preached "being where your feet are." Colby loved Grandpa Owen, and Grandpa Owen loved Colby.

That is how life was for Colby until he left for college at eighteen. One week he spent with Grandpa Owen, stocking shelves at the grocery store, watching baseball games (Grandpa Owen had been a college pitcher), and attending church. The next week he spent riding around with Grandpa Wright in his old Dodge, working on his little farm, and listening to one of his many stories.

The honeymoon ended within the first five minutes of the first faculty meeting with his high school teachers and staff. Colby had just finished introducing himself and was reviewing expectations for staff when the metaphorical wedding cake went bad.

To be fair, the teachers at Kinney didn't know Colby—but they weren't very interested in giving him a chance. When Colby began talking about the teacher dress code, an issue brought up by Superintendent Yates in the interview process, Mr. Harrison, the world history teacher, interrupted.

"Mr. Owen, we have students who rarely come to school, and when they do, they are late and barely dressed. Shouldn't we talk about that instead?"

Colby took a deep breath as the air went out of the rest of the room. Fifty staff members looked at him, many with little kindness or empathy in their eyes. It was evident that many approved of what Mr. Harrison had said.

The rest of the meeting carried on without any more questions or outbursts from the faculty, but the tone was set for what would be a challenging year.

Two months in, Colby began to wonder if he was cut out for his position. While the first faculty meeting had not been the experience he was hoping for, he had begun to understand and empathize with what his teachers felt. Low expectations from previous campus administration had conditioned the students to believe that not taking school seriously was okay. The parents seemed ambivalent at best. Those who made the effort to come to school for meetings about their children were easily offended and grew defensive if anyone brought up student behavioral or academic concerns. The teachers, while not openly defiant, resisted most ideas generated by Colby and his new assistant principals. Finally, Colby had already been called in twice by Dr. Yates because board members had questioned her about the "new guy at the high school."

On a bright and cool afternoon in early October, Colby decided to spend an afternoon with Grandpa Wright, ostensibly to while away an afternoon fishing with his gregarious grandfather on one of his three stocked catfish ponds. What Colby really wanted was some advice from one of the men he trusted most.

When Colby walked into the ranch-style house, he was met with a bear hug that almost squeezed the life out of him. Though older now, Grandpa Wright had lost none of his enthusiasm for seeing his grandson. Since Colby had left for college over ten years earlier, his busy new career as a teacher-coach, and later an assistant principal, had cut into their time together. Yet Colby knew Grandpa Wright was proud of who he had become.

They chose the catfish pond that was the easiest for grandpa to get into and out of. All the ponds were stocked well; a man that liked to eat like Grandpa Wright wouldn't have settled for less. But the pond they decided on was the only one with a pier that had a step-down stair into a waiting aluminum boat. This ease of access made the pond more appealing to a man in his seventies who was a little on the heavy side.

The calm air and the water that was partially clouded from rain the previous evening made for perfect conditions; before long Colby felt they were doing more catching than fishing. They pulled one catfish after another into the boat, and they fell into the old habit of tracking who was catching the most and who had the heaviest sack of fish. Grandpa Wright had raised Colby to believe that competition made everything better.

Eventually, the conversation slowed down the fishing; focusing on the bobber was hard when Grandpa Wright was on a roll. His stories were often peppered with questions for whoever was listening, making it difficult for them to attend to other matters. Questions like "What would you have done?" and "Can you believe that?" didn't require an answer, but they did engage listeners. Colby just smiled and nodded, which of course encouraged Grandpa Wright to keep laying it on.

After a while, Grandpa Wright got around to asking Colby about the new job, and Colby didn't hold back. He and Grandpa Wright had always been an honest pair, and years in the construction business had taught Grandpa Wright, and by association Colby, that time was money and getting to the point was the most profitable way of doing business. So, Colby didn't mince words.

"Grandpa, I don't know if I am cut out for this job. It's been one thing after another since I started." Colby listed all the challenges facing him. He touched on the teachers, the students, the parents, the superintendent, and the board members. Grandpa Wright listened attentively. When Colby told the story of Mr. Harrison and what he said at the first faculty meeting, Grandpa Wright actually smiled, though Colby didn't see anything funny about it.

"Colby," Grandpa Wright began, "why did you interview for the job in the first place? Sounds to me like you knew it wouldn't be all roses and unicorns going in."

"That's true, Grandpa," Colby said. "I knew it would be tough, but I believed that if I arrived early, stayed late, and brought energy each day, they would eventually come around to my way of thinking. Didn't you always tell me the early bird gets the worm? Right now, I feel like the worm."

Grandpa Wright chuckled. "You still haven't answered the question," he said.

"I interviewed because I was excited to make a difference. You and Grandpa Owen have always made it clear why education is important, and I believe it too. Education opens doors."

Grandpa Wright nodded in agreement and set his fishing pole down.

"I had a foreman once." He spoke in that baritone voice he used when telling a story. "He was bright, young, full of energy.

He was one of those who, if you asked him to jump, would say, 'How high?' He was skilled too. He could rough a house in and finish it out. No problem was so big, no detail so small that he couldn't figure out the cheapest, quickest, best way to handle it. On top of that, he had character; he wouldn't have stolen from a job if you told him stealing was part of the job."

Grandpa paused, then said, "I had to let go of him by the end of the first year."

Colby couldn't believe what he was hearing. He knew his grandpa had high expectations and demanded a lot from the people who worked for him. He also knew Grandpa Wright had fired many over the years, but he had never heard, or believed, that such an employee could lose his job working for his grandpa. Colby knew how much his grandpa valued the characteristics of the foreman.

"Why?" he asked.

"I had to let him go," Grandpa said, "because his crew wouldn't work for him. No matter how good that foreman was, he couldn't do the one thing I had hired him to do, which was lead. And to lead, you must show your people that you care."

Colby was stung by the last thing his grandpa said and felt his cheeks burn with embarrassment.

"I do care, Grandpa! I'm the first one there, and I'm the last one to leave. I take on all problems that are given to me, and I don't stop until I have them figured out. When I go home in the afternoon, I'm drained. I don't know how I can give any more."

"Colby, I know you care. But do they?" He paused for an answer, and hearing none, continued.

"Your Grandma Gloria was a great woman. I miss her every day, and I know you do too. I loved her with all my heart, but if I had never said it or showed it, she may not have believed it. I can be a hard man to love, believe it or not." Grandpa winked when he said that, and Colby had to smile. He had seen firsthand how unlovable Grandpa Wright was when it was necessary for him to deliver one of his famous "get-right" speeches to the unfortunate crew that had drawn his ire.

Grandpa Wright continued. "I learned from your grandmother that showing you care is the grease that makes the engine go."

Colby had his grandfather's stubborn streak, and he wasn't quite ready to accede. "Grandpa, they should know I care by my actions. Didn't you always say actions speak louder than words?"

"You listened close, didn't you?" Grandpa Wright said with a grin. "You're right, I did say that, and it is true. Your words don't have much meaning if you don't walk the talk. Caring, though, is an investment you make in your people on a personal level. As a leader, you have to make that investment. Your people are your greatest asset."

"I know that," Colby said, yet he knew he was missing something.

"When you were a little guy, you rode with me to job sites. Did you ever think it odd that we usually visited the crews around lunchtime?"

Colby thought back, and he began to see what Grandpa Wright was getting at. His grandfather made sure to spend time with his construction crews, and lunch was the best time to catch them when they were all together.

"Those men," Grandpa Wright said with some emotion in his voice, "are the only reason we have this catfish pond to fish in right now. Everything our family has is because of them. On the other side of the coin, they counted on me to keep them working so they could provide for their families. We were in it together, and because of that, I knew where my people were from, the names of their kids, and their favorite beverages, which I always left a six-pack of in their truck on their birthdays."

He guffawed so loudly and with so much force at the last thing he had said that his shaking body mass threatened to send them both into the chilly water.

When the boat steadied and the threat of falling in subsided, Colby began to realize he had failed to show his people how much he cared. He had neglected his greatest resource, his teachers. Without them, Kinney High didn't have a prayer.

Colby had one more question. "Grandpa, did you ever think about getting rid of the crew instead of the foreman? I mean, they made the choice not to work for him. Wouldn't it have made sense to keep a guy like that around?"

Grandpa picked up his rod and reel out of the bottom of the boat and, after threading a worm on the hook and casting his bobber next to an inviting bit of shade under some willow trees, said, "Son, you're right. I could have fired that crew and kept the man. But do you know what would have happened? He would have hired another crew, and soon he would have been in the same boat again. You can't force someone to care; it has to be real."

Colby nodded. He understood now. He knew he cared, but if his people didn't, it wouldn't matter. His teachers couldn't follow him around all day and see the work he was putting in. He had to go to them.

"One last thing," Grandpa Wright said as Colby sat there mulling his next steps with his staff. "Do you remember who my favorite president was, and why?"

Colby quickly and correctly replied, "George Washington, because he always told the truth." Grandpa Wright had extolled the virtues of truth for as long as Colby could remember.

Grandpa Wright grinned and nodded in affirmation.

"Good memory. When I was considering what to do with the foreman, I thought about one of President Washington's quotes, and it helped guide me to the decision I made. Honest George once said that it's better for a lion to lead an army of asses than for an ass to lead an army of lions."

Colby knew what his beloved grandpa was going to say next, so he beat him to the punchline: "I see what you're getting at. Colby, don't be an ass."

Once again the quaking of laughter from inside the boat threatened to throw them both in.

Chapter 2

An Author's Reflection on Care

Any leader taking on a new role knows the excitement that comes with new opportunities and challenges. I certainly do! Every one of my chances to lead began with great expectations and starry eyes. I always had the same vision: my leadership tenure would leave an indelibly high mark that my successors would struggle to meet! The night before my first day was always sleepless, as I thought through every little thing that could go right and wrong. I still have trouble sleeping before students and teachers arrive for their first day, and I've been in school leadership positions for almost fifteen years. The feelings that come with assuming a new leadership role are akin to those experienced at the beginning of a roller coaster ride; a great deal of excitement, a little fear, and the anticipation of unexpected twists and turns on the coming journey.

That's part of the fun, though. While we may at times rue the challenges that confront us, as leaders we must also understand that those challenges and experiences give wisdom. Benjamin Franklin's succinct advice that "pain instructs" underscores the value of experience, no matter how painful. The trials we endure as lifting leaders are inevitable and necessary.

The lifting principal chooses to take the risks involved in caring, coaching, and courageously challenging teachers to be their best. As a lifter of others, I've received my share of scars, many of which were inflicted by those who didn't want to be lifted.

In *The Obstacle is the Way*, author Ryan Holiday quotes Marcus Aurelius, a Roman emperor and Stoic, who maintained that "The impediment to action advances action." Aurelius first, and Holiday after, argue that what stands in our way can actually help us get our way. They say this is true because our obstacles help us:

- Develop the urgency needed to change.
- Make our plans better.
- Initiate creative thinking and problem solving.
- Reaffirm why what we are attempting to do matters.

Your ability to lift depends on your ability to see and accept the obstacles in your path. Lifting is not easy; it is only for those who truly want what is best for the people in their organization. As Colby's story shows, for many principals the greatest impediment is often the very people they try to help!

Colby knows turning around Kinney High School will be tough, but he is excited. You should be excited to lead as well! Not everyone is chosen. Colby views obstacles as opportunities. You should too. As a leader, you'll find that no problem brought to you will be an easy fix; otherwise, someone would have already easy-fixed it. I encourage you to embrace those problems and be proud you are the one delegated to make them right. If you don't or can't, who will?

Two problems confront Colby in these first few pages. They are the same problems that confronted me as a new lifting leader and, to be honest, still confront me today as a veteran lifting leader:

- How do I persevere through the hard days?
- How do I show that I care?

A big part of persevering through the hard days is grit. Grit comes from many places, depending on who you are. We all have different things that make us tick. My grit comes from an innate competitive drive. Everything is a competition to me, and I am naturally motivated to win. As Marcus Aurelius said, "If something is humanly possible, it is attainable by you too." The deciding factor that made me apply for and get my first job as a school superintendent was the simple observation that I could do what I saw other superintendents doing, but better. Was that ego or naïveté on my part? Probably both. What can't be disputed is what I felt when I made that decision to go for it.

Resiliency, a positive attitude, and a good stubborn streak also contribute to grit. Every leader is different; it is your prerogative to determine where your grit comes from and learn how to unleash it when necessary. As a leader who lifts, you will need your grit to always be available, often at a moment's notice.

Persevering through hard days requires leaders to access their "why" at a moment's notice. The "why" is the reason you do what you do. Mine is an almost maniacal belief in the power of education and what it can do for the life arc of underprivileged youth. Education has opened doors for me that would not have existed otherwise, and because of that fact, I have seen and done many things my parents never could, and my children have advantages I never did at their age. I want the same for other kids. When I have a bad day, that "why" always whispers, "It's worth it."

Find your why, and you will find a way to persevere through the inevitable hard days as a leader who lifts.

As Colby learned, a leader must earn the right to lift, and the first step to earning that right is showing care. That to show care a leader must act authentically in caring ways is an intuitive truth, but worth stating explicitly. Going through the motions without any real investment is a trap we must all avoid. Lesser leaders always get outed; sooner or later, they are revealed to be inauthentic, agenda-driven, and fake. Such a perception makes trust impossible. Lifting leaders can't operate without trust.

So how do you genuinely care for all your teachers? I'm sure you can identify teachers with whom you have interacted in the past or who work on your campus now who are somewhat unlovable. Differing personalities, attitudes, belief systems—these things can sometimes push us apart from the very people we rely on most.

Empathy and respect enable me to show authentic care for principals and teachers. Empathy is the ability to understand and share the feelings of another, while respect is a feeling of admiration for the qualities of another. These two qualities allow me to get past superficial issues and effectively develop the care I need to earn the right to lift.

Empathy is not easy for me. I am old-school in that I believe everyone has a job to do, and the paycheck and the intrinsic value of a job well-done are rewarding enough. I do appreciate a kind word, but it isn't what drives me. I had to slowly get past my self-centeredness and come to understand that not everyone is like me. This was a huge leadership blind spot for me, as self-evident as it may seem. I have, however, been a principal, and I understand the challenges that come with that job. That perspective helps me empathize with the principal's position much of the time, even though it may be at odds with my own. Having walked in another's shoes greatly promotes empathy. The best teachers remember being students, the best principals remember being teachers, and the best superintendents remember being campus principals.

Teachers are the biggest variable influencing whether students achieve academic success or not. This fact alone demands that principals have respect for the role teachers play in the school. From time to time, the principals who report to me will vent about their teachers. I'll listen and nod understandingly, but if it goes on too long, I remind them of what the research says about the vital part teachers play in the academic development of students. Real problems must be fixed, but principals can never allow themselves to forget how much students need great teachers in their classrooms.

Grit and a clear understanding of the "why" behind the work allow lifting leaders to persevere through the hard days they must have to gain wisdom. Empathy for teachers and respect for the important work they do each day help the most unsympathizing principals appreciate even the most unlovable teachers.

Chapter 3

Showing Care

Colby cared, but he realized after the fishing trip with Grandpa Wright that unless he showed it, his people might never know. Kinney High and his leadership role couldn't afford to take that chance.

Colby reprioritized. Instead of focusing on programs, he would focus on people. Instead of dedicating his time to paperwork, he would do people-work.

He went to his lead teachers (including Mr. Harrison) and had thorough sessions, his goal being to listen to and serve his teachers. Colby knew that Mr. Harrison had told the truth at that first faculty meeting; the issues he touched on were real. Sometimes critics are the most reliable source of truth, and Colby sacrificed some of his pride and let himself be open to what his teachers had to say.

Through those dialogues he learned one big thing: the teachers did not know the work going on behind the scenes. Many of the concerns about attendance and behavior were being addressed, but because Colby hadn't communicated the work being done, his teachers had assumed it wasn't happening.

Colby made a commitment to his lead teachers to communicate better. The teachers would feel informed and "in the loop," and Colby would be assured that the teachers saw how hard he was working to serve. Before the talk with Grandpa Wright, he would have felt such efforts were self-aggrandizing, but now he knew how vital it was to show that he cared.

Colby redoubled his efforts to get to know his teachers and staff. He was intentional about visiting teacher lounges during lunch. He began writing thank-you notes for the teachers he saw going above and beyond. He put all his teachers' and staffs' birthdays into his phone and made sure one of the first things he did each day was text birthday wishes. Colby was an early riser, so those birthday wishes from him were one of the first things his people saw on their special days.

Colby's commitment to care extended beyond his teachers and staff to his students. Now understanding how important communicating that care was, Colby organized class meetings at the end of each six-week grading period. The primary purpose of the class meetings was to celebrate good things students were doing and give praise for progress. Colby and his assistant principals worked hard to make these class meetings special for the students. They produced slideshows of student accomplishments from the prior six weeks, hosted gift card giveaways for perfect attendance and behavior, and guided each class through team-building exercises. Through those class meetings the principals got to know their students and the students got to know their principals.

By Christmas, Colby felt that his and his assistant principals' efforts at building relationships were being well-received, so they continued the work on people-building through the spring. It wasn't hully-gully either; the expectations that Colby set at the beginning of the year had put professional boundaries in place that, in combination with his efforts to show care, by April had Kinney High seeming like a place staff and students wanted to be.

And then, the scores from state testing came back.

As Colby traveled the five minutes across town for his appointment with Dr. Yates, he reflected on the feelings he had when he had first seen the test scores the previous day. He had felt sick in his stomach. He knew the results would invoke a call from Dr. Yates. More importantly, he knew those scores would indicate to Dr. Yates and others the success of his leadership, or more accurately, the lack thereof. There was no way around it. The academic results of his high school students placed the entire school district on dangerous ground, and he would be the one teachers, students, parents, and board members would look to for answers. They would have to wait, because his boss, Dr. Yates, was first in line.

Grandpa Owen had always told Colby that things were never as good or bad as one might think going into a situation. As it turned out, his grandfather was right in this situation. When Dr. Yates hired Colby, she told him the job would have many challenges. She also told him to expect a learning curve;

just as it had taken time for the high school to get into its current predicament, so it would take time to reverse that trend and obtain results that satisfied the state.

She was honest with Colby but also kind. She applauded the effort he had given building rapport with staff and students, and she praised his work ethic. Nobody could say Principal Owen had fallen short in that department.

Dr. Yates encouraged Colby, but she also clearly explained where Kinney High School stood. She could justify the year's results to the board members. A new principal and new assistant principals meant that it was fair to allow them a year of observation to diagnose problems and develop solutions. By year two, though, a plan had to be put in place and some positive results seen so that stakeholders could be assured that Kinney High School was heading in the right direction.

Colby called a faculty meeting and perceived immediately that word of the scores had reached the ears of his teachers. The looks in their eyes told him they were discouraged and uneasy about what their leader was about to say to them. The atmosphere was certainly different from that of Colby's first meeting with them back in August.

In that meeting, he did what he knew he must. He was honest and kind, much as Dr. Yates had been with him. He owned the results, saying many times that he had to do better. In Medieval parlance, he fell on the sword.

He spoke to his staff about controlling the controllables. The scores were the scores; little could be done about that. The team could, however, use that information to fuel their efforts going forward. He promised his teachers he would produce a plan soon, and he expressed excitement about what the next year would bring.

The body language of the teachers changed, and the mood of the room transformed from defeated to somewhat hopeful. Colby didn't know it, but this meeting to discuss spring test scores was far different from the meetings held by his predecessors. The veterans in the room had endured past spring meetings; they had expected to be shouldered with the blame and mandated to "do better."

Colby's humility and grace in that moment did a great deal to convince even the most skeptical teachers that they finally had a leader that truly cared about them.

Work had to be done though, and Colby knew the clock was ticking. He had never felt more urgency than he did right then. The problem was that he wasn't sure what his next move should be, and time was not on his side; he had one, maybe two years to effect positive change on a campus that hadn't seen it in quite a while.

Colby decided it was time to call on Grandpa Owen.

Chapter 4

The Obstacles to Caring and the
Consequences of Not Showing Care

The First "C" to Lift: Caring

Lifting is a formula with three ingredients: caring, coaching, and courage. The absence of one of these crucial pieces limits or completely destroys the ability of leaders to push for progress and elevate the performance of those around them. Caring without coaching and courage only maintains the status quo. Care and courage without coaching is unfair and frustrates employees ("How can you expect me to do what you want if you haven't trained me?"). Coaching without care leads to tone-deafness and, in extreme cases, defiance. Care and coaching without courage make progress optional. The three Cs of Lifting are also sequential; for example, coaching before caring makes the coaching far less effective than it could have been if care had preceded it.

Lifting is an intentional effort to help people be their best selves. A wise leader knows the success and vitality of any organization resides in the collective power of its employees to be and do their best. Not all forms of leadership are of equal level; some are above or below others. Lifting leadership is the highest, and it takes special leaders to reach that summit.

Obstacles to Caring

John Wooden said, "I worry that business leaders are more interested in immediate results rather than having the patience to build up a strong organization, and a strong organization starts with caring for their people." As Wooden noted, it takes time and patience to build a strong organization. Caring is not a task that leaders ever finish; it continues throughout the process of lifting.

As Colby learned, moving too fast can produce resentment and distrust. It has been said that the word "love" is spelled T-I-M-E. Before people will believe what their leader says, they must believe in who the leader is.

Sometimes, leaders take jobs for the wrong reasons. While making more money is a nice thing, it can't be the only reason they signed up to do the job. Internal forces move people far more effectively than external forces, and lifting leaders cannot allow themselves to accept the responsibility of leading unless they know their "why." That "why" powers leaders through the hard days.

Knowing the "why" allows leaders to verbalize it when necessary, and followers need that at times. Grandpa Wright was adamant that Colby needed to "show his care." We show care through our words and actions. When our words and actions line up and indicate the same thing—that "I am here for the right reasons"—our followers begin to believe. A leader cannot lift without care. Leadership that sticks, that leaves a legacy of change, requires leaders who model an ethics of care.

Those who serve others make the best leaders, but some leaders, unfortunately, live only to serve themselves. Selfish leaders can hide their personal agendas for a little while, but their true motivations will eventually expose them. When followers see leaders who are in it for personal gain, trust is broken. Broken trust between leaders and followers is often irreparable.

Another obstacle preventing leaders from caring as much as they should is the fear of failure. One of the scariest parts of leadership is putting oneself out there. Most leaders with any experience have felt the pain of showing care only to receive apathy or hostility in response. Leaders, sometimes unaware of themselves, will hide behind a protective shield that prevents them from opening up too much; lifting leaders have warrior hearts and understand that failure is a necessary step toward success. Fully investing in lifting leadership requires plenty of confidence and courage. The risk is high, but the rewards are great!

To summarize, obstacles to care include:

- Moving too fast.
- Leading without an internal "why."
- The inability to effectively show care.
- Serving oneself over others.
- The fear of failure.

Consequences of Not Caring

Not caring has consequences. Leaders who choose not to care cannot lift. Uncaring leaders will be met with indifference, distrust, or outright hostility, attitudes that prevent leaders from leveraging the potential of their followers.

An uncaring leader does not inspire loyalty. Who would give their all for an aloof leader who shows no interest in the lives of employees? To get love, leaders have to give love. Uncaring leaders will find making lasting change doubly difficult. "I say, you do" may get apparent results from surface-level change, but long-term systemic change requires a community effort, whether that community be a business, church, school, or family. Good change always elicits challenges. Successful change in schools usually depends on how open teachers are to the change. With the support of a committed team of teachers and administrators, significant changes can endure both internal and external challenges.

Uncaring leaders rely on the power of their position to incentivize followers. Fear, not loyalty, drives those beneath them. This method of leadership may be enough to get the perfunctory work of the organization accomplished, but it requires the constant supervision of followers to ensure the leader's designs are carried out. Such surveillance demands much of the leader's time and energy.

Finally, leaders need grace. Leaders who are willing to take risks will make mistakes. Uncaring leaders may find their failures weaponized against them by resentful followers. In contrast, caring leaders who build relationships with their followers aren't as afraid to fail because they know their followers trust them.

To recap, the consequences leaders accept when they choose not to care include:

- Difficulty inspiring loyalty.
- Difficulty effecting lasting change.
- Difficulty ensuring the supervision necessary to make leading with fear work.
- Losing relationships based on mutual trust and grace for failure.
- Losing the opportunity to be a lifting leader.

Can you really accept the consequences of not caring?

Lifting Leaders Need to Evaluate Their Care

To lift, leaders must choose to care. Aspiring lifting leaders should ask themselves the following questions:

- Why do I lead?
- Why do I need my employees to follow me?
- Why do I care about the progress of the organization?
- Do my employees know I care about them?
- How can I show I care?
- Does the way I budget time reflect the amount of care I have for my employees?
- How will the achievement of organizational goals benefit my employees?

- Do I hurt as a leader when my employees are unsuccessful?
- Do I know my employees well enough to have conversations with them about topics other than work?
- How much do I value my employees knowing *why* they are doing what is expected of them?
- Can I empathize with the challenges my employees face at work?
- Do my actions line up with my words?

Motivational speaker and author Jon Gordon says that "caring is a success strategy." Leaders cannot elevate others without heart. Just like the foreman Grandpa Wright had to fire, leaders who have all the skills in the world yet lack the cooperation of their followers cannot effectively move an organization in a positive direction. Lifting leadership requires that leaders deeply understand the collective values and desires of their followers. Leaders who are clearly only interested in their own agendas and their own advancement will lose the voluntary cooperation of their followers.

One Last Thing About Caring

All the lifting leaders I have ever known have loved their jobs! As Gordon says, those leaders always looked at their work as a "get to" and not a "have to." That attitude makes all the difference!

PART II

COACHING

Chapter 5

The Elements of Coaching

When Colby walked into C & C Grocery, he smiled at the scene before him. Grandpa Owen, surrounded by three high school students, was delivering a lesson on sacking. Colby approached as closely as he could without being noticed. His grandpa was focused; Colby didn't want to interrupt or distract him.

"So, Jaime, why is it important to keep your hand on the bottom of the sack, especially when you have canned goods in there?" Grandpa Owen asked.

Jaime replied, "To keep the bag from ripping."

"That's right" Grandpa Owen said. "What consequences do we choose if we don't hold the bottom of the bag?"

One of the other teenagers raised his hand.

"Go ahead, Ray."

Ray answered, "The consequences include bad service, unhappy customers, damages to products, and Mr. Owen's disappointment."

Colby nodded his head, grinning. He couldn't count how many times his grandpa preached to him growing up that it wasn't the choices one chose, but the consequences of those choices. Over the years, Grandpa Owen conditioned him to believe that choices had consequences and that taking the time to evaluate those consequences always led to better choices. Colby was pleased to see that his grandfather, at the age of seventy-four, still had the vigor and snap to keep imparting his sage advice. Colby needed some.

"That's exactly right, Ray," Grandpa Owen said. "All three of you are the last people our customers see each time they visit, and we want them leaving with a good experience so they come back. I appreciate the important job each of you do. Have a great day."

Grandpa Owen dismissed each one of his young subjects with a handshake and sent them on their way.

He noticed Colby standing nearby after the sackers departed.

"Colby!" he said. "What are you up to today?"

All of a sudden, Colby felt a little sheepish. Here he was on a Saturday morning, bothering his grandpa while he took care of business. Further, Colby wasn't there just to say "hello"; he was there because he felt he was failing as a leader and needed advice from the man who had done so much to help him improve as a leader. Colby almost felt that by asking for advice, he had failed to apply the teachings of his grandfather.

"I, um, just wanted to come by and talk for a few minutes, but I can see you're—" Before he could finish the sentence, his grandpa had already grabbed his arm and pulled him along.

"Walk with me." Even at seventy-four Grandpa Owen was so fit, so agile, that few people could keep up with him, especially when he was on a mission. "We can talk. Just hang with me for a few minutes. I have to check on a few things."

Colby fell in behind his grandpa as he made a beeline to the pharmacy. "Mrs. Duplichain, how is our new call-out system working today?" Grandpa Owen asked an employee behind the counter.

Mrs. Duplichain, the lead pharmacy technician, smiled and responded, "Fine, Mr. Owen! We got the report this morning. Currently, sixty-eight percent of yesterday's prescriptions have been picked up, and it isn't even eleven yet!"

"Well, that is fine, Mrs. Duplichain!" Grandpa Owen exclaimed. "Remember what the trainer said. If we aren't at seventy-five percent by noon, call the support line to make sure there were no glitches with the automated dialing system."

The pharmacist nodded. "Yes sir. I have a note right here. I will let you know what they say if we have to call."

Grandpa Owen gave her a thumbs up and a smile, then moved toward the back of the store where the loading dock was located. As they walked, Grandpa Owen informed Colby that he had a new lead stocker. He had made a point to check on the new employee once a day until the young man settled into a productive routine.

That visit completed, it was off to the business office, where Grandpa Owen got his daily update of the previous day's receivables from Mrs. Boyette, his business manager. After glancing at the previous day's receipts, Grandpa Owen grumbled, "Still five percent behind Store #4 for the month."

The two finally settled into Grandpa Owen's orderly and clean office. All manner of baseball memorabilia adorned the two upright shelves behind his rolling chair and tidy desk. When Colby was young, Grandpa Owen gave him his own desk in the back left corner of the office. While his grandpa returned calls or did paperwork, Colby pretended that he was the assistant manager. Grandpa gave him a daily agenda of errands and tasks to perform, and before it was time to go home, a seven-year-old Mr. Colby Owen stood before the great man and gave the day's report.

Grandpa Owen listened intently, often with the slightest wrinkle of a grin on the right corner of his lips, as Colby launched into his summary of the day's events. Properly lining up the grocery carts, ensuring the freezer thermometers were set precisely to twenty-nine degrees Fahrenheit, and thoroughly cleaning the carpets at the entryways took on the utmost seriousness and gravity during Colby's reports. If Grandpa Owen felt he had performed solid work, he handed Colby a crisp one-dollar bill and firmly shook his hand. Rarely, if ever, did Colby leave the grocery store without one of Grandpa Owen's dollar bills in his pocket.

Sitting in the same office, Colby reflected that his Grandpa Owen had always made him feel worthy and confident. Grandpa had always made him feel that his presence in the store, even as a seven-year-old boy, was important.

Colby was jolted out of his thoughts by his grandfather's voice.

"Is it true your scores didn't come back the way you wanted them to?"

Of course he would know, thought Colby. He had shared everything with Grandpa Owen, from his joy at getting the job, to his initial challenges, to the advice acquired from Grandpa Wright, to his renewed efforts at showing his staff how much he genuinely cared.

"Yes sir." That was all Colby could say. His grandpa obviously had the scoop. There was no sense in saying something that would muddy the waters or risk giving the impression he blamed the results on anyone but himself. Grandpa Owen did not approve of leaders who skirted accountability.

After a pause, Grandpa Owen asked, "What do you have that works?"

Apollo 13 was a movie they both loved and had watched together many times. The NASA Commander in the movie asked that question during one of the bleakest moments of the Apollo 13 space shuttle mission.

Colby returned the grin his grandpa was giving him because he knew exactly what Grandpa Owen was getting at. Colby's mission was in peril, and this was his grandpa's clever way of helping him stay positive.

"Well, the teachers and staff know I care. I've worked hard to build their trust in me; they know I'm there for the right reasons."

"That's good, Colby," Grandpa Owen replied. "Your people will make you or break you, and you don't have anything if you don't have them. What else is working?"

Colby thought for a moment, then noted that his boss, Dr. Yates, seemed to like and support him. He described his assistant principals, relating that they were loyal and hard-working.

Another pause. Grandpa Owen asked, "Anything else?"

"No sir, I think that is about it."

Grandpa Owen leaned forward and asked, "What about you?" Before Colby could answer, Grandpa Owen continued, "Colby, what do you think it is I do here?"

Colby grew up in the store following his grandpa around, watching him, and working for him; the question should have been easy to answer, but words left him in that moment. Colby's silence encouraged Grandpa Owen to answer his own question. "I am a coach."

Seeing Colby's confusion, Grandpa Owen explained, "A coach teaches, encourages, inspires, and, most importantly, plays to win. Everyone wants to win or be part of an organization that wins. The coach's job, his promise to his team, is to put them in the best position to be successful. Just because this is a grocery store doesn't mean I don't come to work each day trying to win. There might not be a giant scoreboard in left field, or striped base paths, or a pitcher's mound, but there is a game being played that can be won or lost every single day."

Baseball was an enormous part of Colby's life growing up with his Grandpa Owen, but he had never considered what he did at Kinney High to be a game, and he sure didn't know what winning looked like on the high school campus. All he knew was that he sat in front of a man whose business had such a good reputation that people from other towns came to it, even though those towns had grocery stores.

"Everyone needs a coach," his grandpa continued, "but before you can coach, your team has to trust that you have their best interest at heart. You have that, Colby. That is what is working."

"Okay." Colby nodded. "I'm starting to get what you're saying, but I'm still confused about what winning looks like at Kinney. I know we could use test scores as the 'scoreboard,' but we are so far behind the curve that I wonder if that's realistic. That would be like the Kinney High varsity baseball team taking on the Yankees."

"You are correct." Grandpa Owen nodded in agreement. "Good coaches don't set their teams up for failure. Good coaches help their teams build confidence, and crushing losses don't beget confidence. If you can't win the big game, your team needs to focus on winning at the things that contribute to winning. What are those things, Colby?"

Colby, in spite of his youth as a leader, had implemented improvement plans at other schools and had the expertise to know what his grandfather was asking for.

"Well, our student attendance is currently last in the county. If kids don't come to school, they can't learn."

Grandpa Owen agreed. "That makes sense. If my customers don't show up, I can't sell anything. What else?"

Colby was on his grandfather's wavelength now, and his observations from a year of working at the high school made the second answer easy.

"Our student management system needs to be tweaked. My assistant principals and I spend too much time in the office dealing with behavior issues. I don't know how right now, but we have to fix that."

Grandpa Owen, eyes twinkling, quickly asked, "What are the consequences of a poor student management system?"

Colby was expertly trained in this line of questioning from years of his grandpa's efforts to help him become a better decision maker. Colby listed the consequences of a broken student management system: students in the office rather than in the classroom learning; increased conflict with parents, teachers, and students; and time spent by his assistant principals and himself in the office rather than in the classrooms, the hallways, and the cafeteria. Colby was already wrestling with that challenge, but the notion that he was a coach in a game to be won certainly put a new, different spin on an old problem.

"One more," Grandpa Owen prodded.

Colby's gears were turning now, and he replied, "Grandpa, we have way more than three things we need to get better at. Can I have a few minutes to jot down a list?"

He was already searching for a pen on his grandpa's desk.

"Whoa, whoa, whoa!" Grandpa Owen put his hands up. "Colby, slow down. Remember, a coach sets the team up for success. What do you think will happen if you try to coach your team on ten different things?"

Colby got the point. While he felt most of his teachers would do whatever he asked, too many demands at once might overwhelm and discourage them.

"Colby, if everything is important, nothing is important. Good coaches know how to prioritize their leadership toward things that will grow their teams the most. They also know that Rome wasn't built in a day."

Colby sat back in this chair. "Grandpa, I know what you're saying, and I know you're right. The problem is that I don't have a lot of time to build my Rome. The clock is ticking; I have to get Kinney High turned around *soon*." The exasperation in Colby's voice betrayed the anxiety and stress he was holding on to, and he could see that Grandpa Owen heard it too.

"Colby, you might not know this, but when I was your age, I had to make the decision to either buy this grocery store from the only man I had ever worked for or find a job elsewhere. Mr. Dowdy was going to sell, and if I didn't buy it, he was going to sell it to someone else who probably would have cleaned house."

Colby was surprised. "I thought you had always owned it."

"At that time, I had a young family. Your daddy, only four at the time, and your grandmother depended on me to make the right decision. I loved and admired Mr. Dowdy, but he had really made a mess of the grocery store in the years preceding his decision to sell, and I knew if I bought it that I would inherit all those problems. I also knew that if I bought the store and I couldn't get it turned around, I would be bankrupt, my good credit would be ruined, and my failure would bring hardship on my family. I suffered through several sleepless nights, wrestling with what decision I should make."

Colby thought it incredible that Grandpa Owen had never told him this story, but he could see by the way his grandfather looked that just the memory of that agony was not something he wanted to revisit regularly. In fact, Colby found himself feeling sorry his problems had forced his grandpa to relive what was obviously a very difficult time in his life.

"Grandpa, you obviously made the right decision. Forty years later, you have the best grocery store for miles around. My question is, why did you decide to take the risk?"

"I took the risk because I believed in myself and my ability to coach my people," he said. More importantly though, I believed that if we got good at winning the things that contributed to the bottom line, like customer service, advertising, and operational efficiency, the bottom line would take care of itself."

"So, if I take care of the little things, I won't have to worry about the big things," Colby said. "Makes sense."

Grandpa Owen nodded. "Like you, I was up against the clock, but I knew there were no silver bullets when it comes to success; greatness takes time. If you work for someone who believes otherwise, maybe Kinney High isn't the place for you. Of course," Grandpa Owen stated matter-of-factly, "you could just quit. There are plenty of jobs out there."

Colby sat up straight in his chair, his temper flaring. "I'm not a quitter, and you know that!"

Grandpa Owen held up his hand. "But I know you won't. You are not a quitter. Forget about the clock and focus on winning at the things that contribute to winning. If you do that, you'll get closer to winning the big game a lot quicker than you think."

Grandpa Owen insisted on walking Colby out to the parking lot. Colby felt lighter, as if the burdens that had saddled him as he walked into his grandpa's grocery store had been discarded somewhere around the frozen food aisle. The idea that his work as a leader was a game to be won resonated with him. He simply had to put on his coaching hat.

As they said their goodbyes, one of the sackers Colby had seen receiving a lesson on the proper way to handle a bag of groceries came out of the store following an older woman. The sacker had a firm grasp on the bottom of the bag and, seeing Mr. Owen, flashed him a big smile full of freckles and braces. Grandpa Owen returned the smile with one of his own, accompanied by a big thumbs-up.

Chapter 6

An Author's Reflection on Coaching #1

As I sat planning the staff development schedule with my group of campus principals the other day, I reflected on what separates schools from other industries and organizations. One reason I enjoy working in schools as a teacher and administrator is that every year contains a beginning, an ending, and an opportunity during the summer to reflect and prepare to do it all better the following year. Though we may have flubbed it up the year prior, we get the opportunity to evolve and apply the lessons from last year's victories and defeats. This yearly quickening empowers teachers and administrators to be better.

Colby, through his tireless work showing his care for his teachers, set himself up to be a lifting leader, although he didn't know it when he walked into Grandpa Owen's grocery store. When followers believe their leaders really want what is best for them, leaders gain the currency of trust. That trust currency is what leaders need to fuel change. Remember, the right to lift is earned; when your teachers view you as their shepherd, you are positioned to be a powerful coach.

We can all remember the best coaches and teachers we have been influenced by. The time they spent with us and the effort they put into making us better versions of ourselves inspired unshakable loyalty and a willingness to listen. Here's the thing, though: these important people made us better, not just because they cared, but also because they were knowledgeable and talented enough to impart the wisdom they held. We value them because they cared *and* because they effectively coached us.

It is not enough to just build relationships. Lifting leaders can discern:

- What skills their followers need to improve.
- How to improve those skills.
- How to create, through the use of data and other means, the sense of urgency that helps individuals see, appreciate, and own the need to change.

Most of a teacher's time is unmanaged, so the best coaching principals know how critically important it is to emphasize the "why" at every opportunity. When teachers agree with and understand the need for a change, students will benefit. Then, it just becomes a matter of how gifted the leader is at coaching.

Here is an activity. On a scale of one to ten (one being a beginner and ten being a master), how do you rank as a coach in the following five areas of teacher development:

- Curriculum (What is taught).
- Instruction (How it is taught).
- Assessment (How learning is measured).

- Intervention (How academic gaps are closed).
- Classroom management (How teachers ensure students attend class and behave).

I believe you can't be honest with others until you are honest with yourself. Do you need to grow in any of the above areas? To maximize the value of your relationship with your teachers, you must be able to coach. Lifting leaders are in the business of growing people; it is your responsibility to become the best coach you can be so your teachers can become everything their students need them to be!

Chapter 7

If Everything is Important . . .

After visiting with his assistant principals and lead teachers and looking at testing data, Colby decided the campus coaching focus would be on student attendance, the campus student management system, and the student academic intervention process. The staff thought other issues needed attention in addition to the three areas Colby decided on, but in keeping with his grandfather's mantra that "if everything is important, nothing is important," Colby held his ground and reiterated Kinney High's commitment to winning at three things that contributed to student achievement.

Colby gathered student attendance results from county high schools to use as his "scoreboard." For his student management scoreboard, Colby had his assistant principals retrieve the last three years of disciplinary referral data. His assistants did some averaging and produced an expected six-week average number of student referrals. They would use this average as a baseline to see whether the classroom management coaching they had given teachers was working.

Last, the student academic intervention process would be scored by the number of student failures every six weeks to determine whether the coaching on how to close academic gaps was working. Once again, Colby and his assistants plowed through the last three years of grade reporting data to determine fair expectations.

During the summer, Colby and his principals used their professional networks to talk with leaders they respected who had successful systems for managing the issues they wanted to target at Kinney High.

Colby was coachable; he knew he had to be if he was going to coach effectively himself. By the time summer ended, Colby and his assistant principals had a game plan for coaching their teachers in the three targeted areas for improvement.

During staff development, campus administrators shared the scoreboards with the teachers. Then, surprising even his assistant principals, Colby pulled out a "Grandpa Owen" special and asked his teachers what the consequences would be for Kinney High if the teachers didn't apply the coaching they were receiving.

It was an engaging, collaborative, enlightening conversation with staff, and the answers to Colby's question poured forth. Easily and with little prompting, the teachers pointed out the serious consequences of not making student attendance, student behavior, and student academic interventions a priority for the school; after all, they had lived with those consequences for years. They saw clearly that a different approach was needed to get a different result.

When staff development was over and the teachers had gone back to their classrooms to make last-minute preparations for the arrival of students the next day, Colby and his assistants gathered in Colby's office to reflect on staff development and make sure all was ready for the first student day.

Colby and his assistant principals were exhausted; coaching was hard work! But they were also excited by the responses of the teachers who saw the value of what they were trying to accomplish as a high school team.

Brenden, the 9th and 10th grade assistant principal, remarked that staff development had gone about as well as it could have.

"I just wish we had thought to take this approach last August," he said.

Thinking about Grandpa Wright and his feelings on how important it was to show care, Colby replied, "Even if we had, coaching without caring would have come off as directive, autocratic, and cold. This August, they know we care and want what is best for them. There are no silver bullets when it comes to winning. It takes work and time, but if we don't have our people behind us we can achieve nothing."

Amanda, the 11th and 12th grade assistant principal, nodded in agreement.

"I don't think the teachers would have received us well if we had come in last August barking orders. Do I need to remind you two of how Mr. Harrison responded to Colby and his teacher dress code announcement?"

All three had a good laugh as they recalled that first meeting over a year ago.

"I do have a question for you though, Mr. Owen," Amanda continued. "You surprised me when you asked the teachers to think of the consequences of not following through with the coaching we gave them. Why didn't you try to sell the three initiatives by focusing on their benefits to teaching and learning? That's what I would have expected."

Colby knew he had chosen his two assistants well; they were loyal, and so the three could be completely honest with one another. Colby had avoided making mistakes with staff, students, and parents more than once because of the counsel of his subordinates. This time, though, he saw a chance to help them grow as leaders.

"For people to change, they must feel the urgency to change," he said. "Knowledge of the consequences of not changing helps provide that urgency."

"I still don't understand why laying out the consequences of inaction is a better way to convince teachers to do some-thing than selling the virtues of the initiative," Amanda said. "I mean, aren't people more likely to buy in to the possibility of positive outcomes than be motivated by the threat of negative outcomes?"

Unfazed by Amanda's push-back, Colby told her, "First, selling implies the customer has the option to buy or not. We aren't attempting to sell our teachers anything. The research is clear that good student attendance, a strong student management system, and an effective approach to student academic intervention are necessary to achieve academic progress for all students. The research speaks for itself.

Colby paused—he saw he was making sense to his assistants.

"Second, we are using this opportunity to develop them and help them learn to be their own coaches." Directing the question to Amanda, Colby asked, "What do you think happens when staff development ends?"

Brenden and Amanda looked at each other and back at Colby, unsure of where he was heading.

"School starts?" Brenden tentatively answered.

"Correct. School starts, and teachers go back to their classrooms to do the job. They are no longer captive to us; they are free to make whatever choices they feel are best. We can't be with them all the time. In the end, our futures as leaders depend solely on whether those teachers we just spent two weeks with practice what we preach when we aren't around."

"That's true," Brenden agreed. "When school starts, we always say we will prioritize getting in classrooms, but then reality hits and the time we thought we would have to monitor instruction disappears."

"That's right," Colby answered. "As coaches, we are supposed to equip our players with tools that will help them succeed. These changes we are implementing will fail or succeed according to our teachers' ability to weigh the consequences of applying that coaching or not. Imagine if they coached themselves without us having to constantly redirect, retrain, and remind them of why we are focusing on these three areas?"

"That would free us up to be a lot more visible," Brenden said.

"Teachers complain a lot about micromanagement," Amanda added. "This could be a tool that gives them more ownership."

Brenden nodded. "This allows them to self-motivate. When the job gets difficult, having a way to refocus is important. On those hard days when it would be easier to let things go, considering the consequences of taking the easy way out might be the thing needed to keep teachers striving for excellence."

"All true," Colby said. "As good as the reasons each of you offered are, neither of you have shared the best part about learning to be your own coach. This skill applies to life outside of Kinney High School. Having a process to improve decision-making can improve the lives of families, churches, and businesses—not just schools. We are the product of our choices. The good and bad things we have in our lives can be traced back to the quality of the decisions we make. This is our chance to give this gift to our people."

By now, Brenden and Amanda had pens out and were taking notes.

Writing with her head down, Amanda said, "Okay, just to be clear, what is the process?"

Colby answered, "First, we don't make choices; we choose the consequences of those choices."

Brenden, a baseball fanatic, said, "So, if you are on the mound with a 1-2 count, you accept the consequences of throwing one in the dirt because you know the hitter may chase it."

"That is correct," Colby told him. "The value of a potential ball is less than the value of potentially striking out the hitter. Good example."

"Thanks, boss." Brenden said.

"Second," Colby continued, "the context of every situation determines the value you place on a consequence."

Brenden and Amanda looked at each other and stared questioningly at him. On the few occasions that Colby truly felt he had the upper hand on his highly intelligent and trusted assistants, he thoroughly enjoyed it. This was one of those times.

Amanda asked, "When you say context, do you mean the current situation?"

Colby nodded in agreement. "That's correct. Consider your baseball scenario, Brenden. What if the hitter you just described is the other team's pitcher, who has never swung a bat before? What if it is the eighth inning, and my arm is ragged out and I don't want to waste a pitch? What if there is a runner on third and the score is tied; do I risk throwing a pitch in the dirt that might get by the catcher? Where is the value in this new context?"

"In that case, there is no way I'd throw that pitch," Brenden said. "I might throw a change or heat outside. Throwing one in the dirt is not worth the risk in that scenario."

Amanda nodded in agreement with Brenden's assessment.

Colby leaned back, hands behind his head. He was pleased that his analogy had helped his assistant principals understand the situational nature of decision-making.

"Agreed. The context completely changed the consequences of your choices. That is why we choose our consequences with every decision we make, and that is why we want to empower our teachers to think through this process themselves. The fact is that we can't be there for every single choice they will be faced with this year. We have to trust and believe in our teachers, because they will be the reason we fail or succeed as leaders. Our futures are in their hands."

Chapter 8

An Author's Reflection on Coaching #2

Leaders have misconceptions, one of the biggest being the idea that they are the normal ones in the room. Normal means "ordinary" or "average." If you are a lifting leader, you are not ordinary or average. The quicker you accept that you will always be the outlier, the better you will become as a lifter of others.

We've all been there as leaders. I prepared, I planned, I rehearsed, I strategized, and I thought about the best way to deliver the information needed to coach my teachers in a particular skill. When the professional development was over, I was pleased and proud of how well it went. I was so sure the learning would stick. And then it didn't.

Just because your teachers have college degrees doesn't mean they will automatically translate your words as a coach into their actions as teachers. They will try, because they believe in you as a person and know that what you suggest is what's best for their students. They will give you everything they have, but do not make the assumption that it will go smoothly every time. Different people learn, interpret information, and view success differently unless a coach commits to walking them through change by:

- Showing them what success looks like.
- Giving them the opportunity to practice.
- Giving them precise feedback when they are successful and when they need to improve.

As lifting leaders, we must commit the time and energy needed to help teachers grow. We have to stay with them. Principals who are the best coaches understand that staff development at the beginning of the year is just that: the beginning. Growth and improvement are a journey. True, some will get it quicker than others—this is an opportunity too. Let those fast-adapting teachers aid you by coaching others when they are ready. We all know as principals that teachers listen a lot more to other teachers than they do to us!

Greatness takes time; there are no quick fixes. Lifting leaders understand that change is an ongoing process and that the teachers they help improve will be better for the thousands of students they will interact with in their careers. A lifting legacy is built, in part, by having that mindset. Looking at leadership that way reveals how vital it is to take coaching seriously.

As an administrator nearing the end of my own leadership journey, I reflect on all the missed opportunities I had to grow teachers. Instead of coaching, I was busy with distractions that seemed important at the time but ultimately proved insignificant compared to the moments of influence I could have had with teachers and students if I had been wiser. If everything is important, nothing is important, and nothing is more important to principals than helping teachers get better.

What I have come to understand is that I worked backward a lot of the time. Those fires I fought as a principal could have been prevented if I had focused on showing my care and coaching my teachers. What were the fires? Student disciplinary issues, angry parents, and poor attendance and test scores. If I had prioritized investing more of my time and energy into lifting teachers, those fires would have dwindled on their own and my teachers would have been better for themselves and their students.

Chapter 9

Coaching to Win

The coaching did not end with staff development. Brenden, Amanda, and Colby continued coaching to win, with a focus that would make even Grandpa Owen proud. It wasn't easy. Implementing the new student attendance plan required help from the teachers, the local judge, and local law enforcement, and while most did a great job and student attendance improved, some feathers were ruffled. Parents and students who had been allowed to slide in the past were now held accountable for chronic absenteeism.

The student management system required work by teachers and principals to train students. No good change comes without challenge; many parents and students were not enamored with the higher standard for student behavior at Kinney High School. Further, some teachers failed to consistently uphold their responsibility to maintain the standard, which made it harder on other teachers who did.

Grandpa Wright always said that on the hard days one had to remember the "why" behind it all. Colby, his teachers, and his assistant principals spent a lot of time that year revisiting "why" it was important for students to come to school each day and behave well while they were there.

The student intervention system was the initiative that created the most conflict between teachers and the campus administration. Some teachers argued that the new system put undue pressure on them to address gaps created by student choices to either do poor work or none at all. The principals listened and did their best to find a middle ground that made sense to teachers and students. As Colby reminded the teachers and his assistant principals over and over, having something in place was better than having the nothing that had been in place for the past several years.

Despite the challenges, Colby and his assistant principals were proud of the work they did supporting their teachers. They were also intentional with teachers and students, challenging them to consider the consequences of the choices they made. They committed to helping teachers and students refine their ability to coach themselves through the challenging situations that emerged throughout the year. While a few teachers and students were reluctant, even defiant, to the implemented changes, the majority at least made an effort to go along. They accepted the coaching because they believed their leaders cared a great deal about doing what was best for them and the school.

Spring student testing came and went, and Colby was eager to learn if the efforts of the high school staff and campus administration had payed off. Colby had a running joke with his high school coaches that it was pure insanity for adults to base their livelihood on what teenagers may or may not do each day. Fair or not, state testing was the final arbiter of the future trajectory of his leadership. That was the game he signed up to play though, and upon reflection, he felt that regardless of the outcome, he had cared and coached the best he could.

Dr. Yates called when the scores came in, as expected. During the phone call, Colby received no indication of whether his visit with her would be good or bad.

Colby walked into Dr. Yates's office with confidence. He was proud of his work. He had controlled the controllables of care and coaching, and he was prepared to accept whatever decision Dr. Yates had to make. She had staunchly stood behind Colby every time a parent, teacher, or board member called to complain about the changes being implemented at Kinney High. She had Colby's respect. He hoped the news she had to share would justify her faith in him.

"Well, Colby," Dr. Yates began, "it's been quite a year."

Colby nodded in agreement.

"When you took this job, I made you keenly aware that it was going to be challenging. You knew what we were facing with the state, and the consequences that would come if we didn't find a way to improve student academic results."

"Yes ma'am, I remember. You were very clear." Colby remembered thinking at times that Dr. Yates seemed to be trying to talk him out of his desire for the position. He couldn't say he wasn't warned.

"You will also remember that student achievement on test scores after your first year continued to regress," she said in a stern tone. "After receiving those scores, we met. At that time, I stated that it was only fair for you to have a year to evaluate Kinney High, but I also stated that it was essential that the students show academic gains after the second year. Time was, and still is, not on our side."

Colby's shoulders dipped, and he exhaled. Kinney High had fallen short again.

"Kinney High has not met the requirements of the state," she said, "but you and your staff are well on your way to changing that." A smile emerged through what had been a stony demeanor. "Colby, your gains are remarkable. Let me be the first to congratulate you." Dr. Yates stood and extended her right hand.

Colby sat there, stunned, before remembering his manners. Then, he jumped to his feet and shook her hand.

As Colby returned to his high school campus, he knew he was grinning. Kinney High had not made the improvements necessary to get out from under the thumb of the state, but he and his collaborators had done enough to give the school a fighting chance to avoid a takeover the following year. While the high school could still fall short, the good news was his staff and students had something to celebrate for the first time in a long time.

After a faculty meeting that included several high fives and fist bumps, Colby retreated to his office. He had shown the gains to his staff, and predictably, the teachers were excited about the progress. The relief they felt was palpable. Colby had reminded the staff of the work done in the last two years. The focus on winning at the things that contributed to winning had put them in position to win the big game.

The euphoria faded as Colby reflected on Dr. Yates's last words in their meeting hours before. She was always kind, but honest too. While the academic gains showed that something was going right at the school, the state was unflinchingly rigid regarding the timeline for schools labeled "Low Performing." With the scores, Dr. Yates had received a letter from the State Commissioner of Education. The letter stated, in very clear terms, that Kinney School District would face a takeover by the state if the academic achievement of students at Kinney High did not reach the required level by the end of the next school year.

Once again, Colby felt the pressure rise. He had cared. He had coached. He had worked harder in year two than he had in year one. Progress felt good, but it would be all for naught if Kinney High fell short in year three. The game seemed stacked against him, and he tossed and turned in bed that night. While his teachers and assistant principals celebrated and rested easy, Colby was haunted by the question, "What's next?"

Chapter 10

The Obstacles to Coaching and the Consequences of Not Coaching

The Second "C" to Lift: Coaching

Everyone needs a coach. Coaches inspire us, encourage us, and bring out our best. We can always better ourselves. Leadership has no destination, no final place at which we "arrive." Leaders are lifelong learners, and lifting leaders chose to develop specific skills related to the needs of their followers.

As we identify areas of improvement for our employees, we can contract with trainers to help us. Those trainers provide services for a fee, and they continue to do so as long as we keep handing over money. Coaches are different. Coaches rely on preexisting relationships. Good coaches are personally invested in our growth and remain so as long as we do our best to apply their coaching. We are much more willing to accept feedback from those we trust, and when we do, we obtain the progress we desire.

Leaders who lift are special because they have the big heart needed to build relationships and they are skilled enough to enhance the growth of their followers. Even leaders like Colby, who may not have the skillset yet, are determined and coachable enough to acquire the needed knowledge to pass along to their employees.

Leaders can certainly coach without having personal relationships with employees. Sometimes this is necessary, but those relational connections maximize employees' openness to feedback.

Obstacles to Coaching

Understanding what obstacles exist to implementing change is crucial. My hope is that if you have read this far, you want to be a lifting leader. Lifting leaders must be coaches that help their followers change for the better. But all good change comes with challenges.

The greatest challenges confronting coaches are their relationships with employees. Building trust takes time, yet sometimes coaching has to occur without a strong foundation of care. Coaching without a foundation of care limits the openness employees may have to trying something new. Because a paycheck is involved in most cases, employees will listen and at least go through the motions of applying the coaching, but such cooperation is forced rather than enthusiastic, based on an awareness of top-down power. Most likely the only motivation employees in such a situation will have to allow the coaching to affect their practices will be external. Lifting leadership works best when internal forces drive the change of the organization. Care is critical to lifting leadership; a lack of care is the primary obstacle to effective coaching.

Another significant obstacle to coaching is a lack of awareness on the part of the leader of what needs to improve. The failure to ask important questions and determine the sources of problems is a serious issue. Only honest leaders can admit things are not going well, and only persistent, disciplined leaders can do the work necessary to track the symptoms to the root causes. Leaders can have great relationships with staff and have the skillset to be a dynamic, effective coach, but if the focus is on the wrong things, problems will not be resolved. This misdirection of effort leads to a lack of results, which hurts principals' credibility with teachers. Colby was effective, in part, because he discerned the initiatives that would contribute most to winning. Lifting leaders must be wise enough to realize that if everything is important, nothing is.

When Colby realized that an effective student intervention process was needed, what did he do? He relied on some of his own experiences, but he also researched schools that were "winning" at that aspect of education. He embraced his role at the high school as the "lead learner" to improve his understanding so he could coach his staff. Lifting leaders accept that they do not know everything—because of that, they are coachable. Because they are coachable, they can be conduits of information that keep the organization energized and healthy. The outside voice of a trainer or a known expert can provide an unbiased view of what is really going on in an organization. Lifting leaders can discern when such viewpoints are necessary. The fact remains, however, that leaders with relationships with their employees are best suited to deliver coaching that will be accepted and acted upon. Leaders who lift may face the obstacle of inexperience, but their natural curiosity and work ethic are generally enough to overcome what Marcus Aurelius called the "impediment to action."

Another obstacle leaders may face is the inability to convey knowledge. Some people are absolutely brilliant in their field but struggle to impart their knowledge to others. For leaders who want to lift, however, good teaching skills are essential. By completely abdicating their responsibility to coach, leaders risk their credibility and miss an incredible opportunity to build relationships with their employees. Aspiring leaders who want to lift must develop a pedagogical aptitude for their field, whether it be related to business, education, church, or family.

Leadership isn't for everyone; people who take too much counsel of their fear cannot lead. Meaningful change does not come without challenge, so leaders, by the job description, repeatedly put themselves in positions where their ideas and beliefs are questioned by followers. Even leaders with fantastic relationships with employees are critiqued and second-guessed when they present new ideas. That is the nature of the beast. Lifting leaders yearn for progress, however, and progress does not come to those who sit idly by hoping for the best. Lifting leaders accept their coaching role and do not allow themselves to be dissuaded by the perceived negativity of a few or the possibility that the needed change will be unpopular. Lifting leaders know that for the organization to be its best, its employees must be their best. Fear or no fear, this requires coaching. Fear is an obstacle many face, but it can be overcome. If the change is worth it, go for it! Nothing ventured, nothing gained!

Let's look again at the greatest obstacles to coaching:

- The lack of relationships with employees (the lack of care).
- The lack of awareness of what needs to be coached.
- The lack of knowledge about what needs to be coached.
- The lack of ability to coach.
- The fear of failure.

Consequences of Not Coaching

Just as leaders who want to lift need to perceive the obstacles confronting them, they need to also recognize the consequences of choosing not to coach.

Lifting without coaching is impossible. Lifting, remember, is elevating the performance of those around you. Leaders who don't coach set their organizations up to regress. Great organizations will become good, then average, then, eventually, subpar. As John Maxwell famously wrote, "Everything rises and falls on leadership." Coaching is a fundamental aspect of leadership, and the second step to the highest level of leadership, lifting leadership.

By electing not to coach, lesser leaders rob employees of opportunities to pursue excellence. Further, such leaders rob themselves of the satisfaction of helping employees achieve their potential. Employees hunger for feelings of success, and success begets success. Failure to have successes today leads to failure to have successes tomorrow. Leaders need, as John Maxwell says, "the Big Mo"; coaching gives the momentum needed to travel from one success to the next. By choosing not to coach, leaders deprive their most important asset, their people, of the success they deserve.

What does it say to you when someone slows down and takes the time to teach you something? Think back on the times people who cared about your success invested their valuable time in your growth. Maybe a parent taught you how to drive a car, or maybe one of your first bosses pulled you aside to share with you an aspect of the business that wasn't in your lane, but part of the big picture you normally weren't privy to. How did those gestures make you feel? Coaching strengthens relationships, and leaders who ignore this truth, no matter the reason, accept the consequences of not investing in their people. Those consequences are far greater than you might realize.

One measure of a leader's legacy is the condition of the organization when the leader departs compared to that when he arrived. The clock is ticking for leaders. That we will all move on at some point is as certain as death and taxes. The question will be, "Did we leave the organization better than we found it?" Lifting leaders always do, partly because they invest in the leadership ability of the employees in the organization. Perceptive leaders can see talent, and that talent often shows up during coaching. Leaders who fail to coach cannot identify those who may be the torchbearers for the organization when they are gone. Do you want to ensure your organization is in a better place when you leave it? Coach your people up, find the ones who shine, and grow them as leaders. You will ensure a strong legacy, and those young leaders will always remember and appreciate the time you invested growing them.

Let's look again at the greatest consequences of choosing not to coach:

- Lifting will be impossible.
- Employees will never experience the level of success they are entitled to.
- The organization will never meet its potential, since its employees won't meet their potential.
- The leader misses opportunities to build relationships and show they care.
- The leader misses opportunities to develop leadership ability within the organization.

Can you really accept the consequences of not coaching?

Lifting Leaders Need to Elevate Their Coaching

To lift employees, leaders must coach. Lifting leaders should ask themselves the following questions:

- What are the systems in your organization that contribute to winning?
- What do you have that works?
- What are three things your staff can improve at that will boost your bottom line the best?
- Do you have a clear idea of what success looks like?
- Do you have a scoreboard to measure yourself against the competition?
- Are your employees open to coaching?
- Have you cared enough?
- Can you effectively explain to your employees the consequences to the organization and their personal success of not getting better in the areas of improvement you have identified?
- Can you effectively coach your people in the areas prescribed?
- If not, what do you have to do to become skilled enough to coach?
- If a skill is beyond your ability to coach, do your people have access to an expert trainer who will take a vested interest in the outcomes of your organization? How can you arrange the relationship with the contracted trainer to ensure that vested interest in a positive outcome for your organization?

One Last Thought About Coaching

The best coaches coach themselves. A great majority of employees' time is unmanaged, so leaders must convince them to make good choices for the organization when they are not around. Just as Colby taught that skill to Brenden and Amanda, we can do so for our employees. We truly are the product of our choices. The choices your people make when you aren't around will dictate the success of the organization you lead. Remember this:

- Every choice has consequences. We choose those consequences.
- The value of every consequence is determined by the context of the situation in which a choice is made.

Coaching your employees on good decision-making not only anchors the organization in sound, logical choices, but also bestows on them a gift that will enrich their lives.

PART III

COURAGE

Chapter 11

The Chair

When Colby arrived at Grandpa Owen's house the following afternoon, he immediately noticed that Grandpa Wright's old Dodge truck sat in the driveway next to Grandpa Owen's gray Forerunner. This was not totally uncommon or surprising; over the years his grandpas had forged quite a friendship. Of course, the timing was somewhat odd. Colby had called Grandpa Owen the day before and asked whether he could come by. "Of course," Grandpa Owen had replied. Knowing how organized and on point Grandpa Owen was, Colby figured it wasn't happenstance that Grandpa Wright was also there at the appointed time.

Grandpa Owen had instructed Colby to come around through the side gate when he arrived. "I'll be in the backyard working on a new project," he had said. Colby did as instructed, and when he eased through the gate, he was greeted with a hysterical sight.

Sanded wood pieces of different shapes and sizes were stacked in neat piles. Wood shaping tools were also in great supply, with different stations set up for what appeared to be the construction of rocking chairs. Three finished products sat in a neat row, with the recently applied dark stain still drying.

The hilarity that Colby was focused on was an argument between his two grandpas. He has closed the gate quietly, so they were not aware that Colby had a front row seat to their raging debate about the durability of one of the chairs.

"Tommy, we won't ever know unless you sit it in it. How can we ever sell our chairs without testing them?" As he spoke, Grandpa Owen had both hands on his hips—the exact same stance he had when lecturing the sackers on the proper way to carry groceries.

Grandpa Wright, not to be cowed, returned fire. "Walter, if you're so confident, why don't you sit your narrow rear end down instead? If it passes muster, I'll consider doing the same. No sense bringing in the tank if it can't hold the golf-cart!"

With a graceful move that reminded Colby that Grandpa Owen had once been quite the athlete, Walter Owen slid into the newly constructed rocking chair and began rocking back and forth, smiling. Grandpa Wright's face reddened while Grandpa Owen feigned a yawn, stretching for effect.

Glowering, Grandpa Wright grabbed the top of his denim overalls and pulled them up while wiggling his backside. This was a sign to anyone that knew the man that Grandpa Wright was vexed, and a vexed Tommy Wright was not to be trifled with. His machinations didn't seem to bother Grandpa Owen; he just kept rocking away.

Three hundred pounds on a light day, Grandpa Wright shooed Grandpa Owen out of the way. Ever so slowly, he eased his massive backside into a chair that, on first sight, didn't seem to have a prayer. Colby held his breath from the shadows, torn between hoping it would hold and hoping it wouldn't. To everyone's surprise but Grandpa Owen's, it held, and did so with minimal creaking. Grandpa Wright was soon rocking away, his apprehension giving way to confidence.

Grandpa Wright was in the process of explaining to Grandpa Owen that it had held only because he had lost a few pounds when Colby emerged from the shadow of the gate, exclaiming "Bravo!" as he clapped his hands and smiled. "Never a doubt!"

"When did you two get into the rocking chair business?" Colby asked, still grinning from what he had witnessed.

"It's a new venture," Grandpa Owen replied as he stepped over a small pile of wood to shake his grandson's hand.

Grandpa Wright gave Colby his signature bear hug, adding, "Building chairs is a lot harder than building houses!"

Colby, as directed by Grandpa Wright, took his turn in the freshly constructed rocking chair. Even though the chair was unfinished, Colby was impressed by its sturdy construction and smoothness of motion. The arm rests were the perfect height, and the slightest curve in the back made the most of the chair's ergonomic function. *These two never cease to surprise*, he thought.

"Congratulations on your scores!" Grandpa Owen said, smiling proudly. "It sounds like you got your staff coached up, and the kids responded!"

Colby, still enjoying the gentle swaying of the chair, replied, "Yes sir, the assistant principals and the teachers really embraced the changes and worked hard. I'm proud of what we accomplished, but we still have work to do."

Colby related his conversation with Dr. Yates to his grandpas. Both listened raptly, grimacing as Colby shared the contents of the letter from the State Commissioner of Education. Grandpa Wright, ever Colby's champion, bristled and said heatedly, "That's about right! No grace from the ivory tower! Let's see that guy do what you have done in the last two years!"

Grandpa Owen, though, saw it differently. "Colby, that letter is a gift." Colby stopped rocking and looked at his Grandpa Owen questioningly. Grandpa Wright was taken off guard as well. Over the years Grandpa Wright, a man that knew people, had come to understand how singularly gifted Walter Owen was. He waited patiently for his friend to explain his thinking.

"Urgency is what you need to effect quick change. That letter does a fine job providing you just that." Grandpa Owen continued, "The hardest situation to make change in is when everybody thinks everything is all right."

Grandpa Wright nodded in agreement. "He's right. People may ignore a few leaks in the ship, but when it begins sinking, they'll hustle."

Colby saw the point, and although he still didn't like the reality of the consequences awaiting the school if it didn't take the final step, he certainly saw how the Commissioner's letter might be of use.

"Okay, I get it. Change requires urgency, and the Commissioner has provided just that. I just don't know what's next. I've given my staff all the support I can; I've cared and I've coached, but it hasn't been enough." He took a deep breath and said in a subdued voice, "I think I've taken the high school about as far as I can."

Looking at his feet, Colby felt beaten. While the chair was comfortable, the way he felt was not. He felt like he was tethered to the ground; his normal boundless energy had left him. He was not a quitter; he would battle, scratch, and claw, doing all he could to get the high school where it needed to be. He just didn't know how.

After a deep breath, Colby looked up, ready to get out of the chair, but before he could, Grandpa Wright put his hands out, indicating that he stay seated.

"Colby, do your staff know you care?" Grandpa Wright asked.

"Yes sir, they do. We worked hard to build relationships after you and I went fishing a few years back. I'm sure they know how much my teachers, my students, and my school mean to me," Colby replied.

Grandpa Owen followed. "Colby, are your staff coached up on what it is you want them to do and how you want them to do it?"

Colby was already nodding. "Yes sir. We worked hard to make sure they know exactly what it is we are trying to do with student attendance, the student behavior management system, and the student academic intervention process. We even worked with them on the decision-making process. Some of my teachers are getting good at coaching themselves," he said. "They may not all agree with what we are trying to do, or how we are trying to do it, but they do know why."

Grandpa Wright nodded at Grandpa Owen, and Grandpa Owen said matter-of-factly, "Colby, sounds to me like you all you have to do now is lift."

"Lift?" Colby asked, curious.

Grandpa Wright weighed in. "What is your greatest resource at Kinney?"

"That's easy," Colby said. "My teachers. They are the number one reason why students succeed or fail. The research is pretty clear on that point."

"Makes sense," Grandpa Wright replied. "Just like my construction crews—nothing would get done without them."

"Just like my grocery store employees," Grandpa Owen said. "If they don't do their jobs, customers won't come back, regardless of how long they have known me."

"Right," Colby agreed.

"So," Grandpa Wright continued, "if your teachers are that important to student success, you need and want them to be their best. That is why you have to lift them."

Colby, impatient for an answer that he couldn't quite grasp yet, blurted, "Can one of you please tell me what lifting means? You two are really cooking my grits right now."

"Lifting," began Grandpa Owen, "means elevating the performance of people around you. Improvement. Progress. The relentless pursuit of excellence."

Colby interrupted, "And I'm *not* doing that? All the caring and coaching I've been doing the last two years hasn't improved Kinney High School? The data say something different!" Colby was fuming.

Grandpa Owen and Grandpa Wright looked at each other, and Grandpa Owen said flatly to Grandpa Wright, "He gets that from you." Grandpa Wright shrugged. He couldn't deny that Colby had seen him throw a fit or two over the years.

Grandpa Owen turned his attention back to Colby. "You have done great work, grandson. Again, there are no magic tricks to attaining excellence. What makes excellence so singular and so rare is that few are willing to do what it takes to achieve it. It takes persistence, grit, positivity, vision, belief, and the doggedness to overcome failure. That is why leadership is so challenging."

Colby nodded in agreement. "It's the hardest thing I've ever tried to do."

Grandpa Owen continued, "It's certainly not for everybody. No one suffers as much as leaders who really chase excellence, because they never rest. They *always* find something to get better at."

Colby had calmed down. He was prone to take things personally, but only because he cared so much. He knew his grandpas understood; they were the same way. "Yes sir, I'm listening."

"Colby, consider that rocking chair you are sitting in. How does it make you feel?"

Colby thought the question random and odd but played along because he knew there was purpose behind it. "Comfortable. Safe. Relaxed. Supported."

Grandpa Owen nodded approvingly. "Good, I'm glad you like it. We worked hard to build that chair so anyone sitting in it would feel those things you just described. It wouldn't be much of a chair if you felt uncomfortable, fearful, uptight, or unsupported in it. It would be hard to enjoy a chair like that." Colby nodded in agreement, still not sure of Grandpa Owen's point.

"What would happen if I pulled that chair out from underneath you?"

Colby instinctively grabbed the handles of the chair. Both of his grandpas were prone to practical joking, and he had learned it was better to be safe than sorry.

"Well," Colby said suspiciously, "I would fall."

"That's right, you would," Grandpa Owen agreed. "Your coaching and caring have given your staff a safe, supporting foundation. That is far better than a shaky foundation, or worse, none at all. Your people trust that you will not let them fall. You should be proud of that, but now that you have created that feeling of support, you have earned the right to lift."

"Earned?" Colby asked.

Grandpa Owen nodded. "Yes, earned. Lifting leaders know they have to earn the right to ask people to be their best selves.

Your teachers, because of your work, caring, and coaching, will accept your insistence on "better" if you have the courage to ask for it. Leaders lift when they provide the right mix of love and accountability. That is lifting leadership."

Colby was listening closely now. He was starting to make the connection between what his grandfather was saying and what it might mean for Kinney High School.

Seeing that his grandson's wheels were turning, Grandpa Owen continued. "Not all leadership is equal, Colby. Lesser forms of leadership tout support, support, support. Support, by its very meaning, is about keeping you from falling. Support does nothing to help an organization rise. Lifting, by contrast, is about taking people from a place of comfort to a place where they become better versions of themselves. That is the type of leadership Kinney High needs right now."

"The rocking chair gave you support and comfort, just as you have for your teachers the last few years." Grandpa Owen looked sincerely into Colby's eyes. "The time and effort spent creating that support was crucial, because now when you decide to offer a hand, they will have to make a decision to take it or refuse. Most will take it because they believe in you. When they do take your lifting leadership, their performance will be lifted. You'll feel your best as a leader when you realize your care, coaching, and courage helped your employees be and feel successful. There really is nothing like it, Colby."

Colby looked at his grandpas, bowed a little by time but still doing all they could to lift him. Colby realized how incredibly lucky he was to have been lifted all his life by the two men standing before him. They had cared, coached, and shown the courage to expect the best of him and hold him accountable even when they had every reason not to. They could have easily spoiled him; both were wealthy and loved him like their own child. They hadn't done that though; they had subverted their own inclinations to demand less because of Colby's circumstances, opting instead to help him be his best. They had disciplined Colby when necessary, and rewarded him for hard work and good choices.

Colby clearly understood now. He was in a position to "lift" the teachers at Kinney High because of the lifting his beloved grandpas had done for him in his youth. Colby felt a new responsibility as a leader. He would go beyond support, working to lift his people to their best. If he did that, the students would benefit. Maybe, just maybe, that would be the thing that saved Kinney.

"What if they don't accept my hand when I try to lift?" Colby asked. He anticipated that a few teachers on his staff, if challenged to be better, would reject his efforts at lifting leadership.

Grandpa Wright answered before Grandpa Owen could. "Because you have cared and coached," he said slowly, "you have earned the right to ask more of your people. Your care and coaching have eliminated the excuses of 'I didn't know' or 'I don't know how.' If they don't give you the effort required or apply the coaching you have given them, they choose the consequences that come with that choice, right Walter?"

Walter nodded and said, "For the few who refuse to be lifted, their choices leave you none."

Colby was standing now, energized and feeling lifted. "I understand now," he said. Colby knew what he and his assistant principals had to do. They had to lift.

Colby and his assistant principals attacked preparations for the coming school year with vigor and enthusiasm. After reviewing the gains made the previous year and considering the gap that remained, Colby, Brenden, and Amanda agreed that improving student attendance, reducing student discipline referrals, and consistently intervening when students struggled academically remained the surest ways to win the game.

The scoreboard would change this time, though. Instead of digging through campus data to establish realistic standards, Colby and his assistants reviewed individual teacher data from the previous school year. They discovered that different teachers had different levels of success in the three areas of focus. Some teachers, for example, were splendid at student management, but their failure reports indicated they needed to improve at delivering student academic interventions. Some teachers needed to get better in all three areas, while other teachers had performed beautifully across the board.

The more Colby discovered about his teachers' strengths and weaknesses, the more excited he became: they had the ability to win the game and prevent the state takeover. They had always been the key. Saving Kinney depended on how effectively the principals lifted their teachers.

Of course, by choosing the hard road of lifting, Colby assumed some risk. Colby accepted the likely consequence that some teachers would not like his expectations of improvement. He and his assistants had to be prepared for those courageous conversations. Nothing less than strong effort and improvement in the areas of focus was acceptable. Colby said many times to his assistants that summer that the greatness of their team would be dictated by how accountable the principals held themselves for the growth of their teachers. If the teachers didn't get better, Colby said the principals would only have themselves to blame.

By the time the teachers came back for professional development in August, Colby, Amanda, and Brenden were committed to elevating the abilities of their teachers. They were ready to lift.

During staff development, Colby and his principals celebrated the previous year's improvement and emphasized that the focus on attendance, behavior, and student intervention was working. Colby unveiled the motto for the year, which was LIFT: Love Inspires Focused Teaching.

Colby asked his teachers why they had chosen education as their life's work. A recurring theme of the answers was that educating was an opportunity to make a difference. Love for the students carried them through the hard days. Colby's motto challenged the teachers to commit their hearts and souls to being the best teachers they could be. They wouldn't have to do it alone either; the principals had worked all summer to develop individual plans for each one of them. By the end of the year,

Colby promised, every teacher would feel the satisfaction of success, of making a difference.

Colby's kindness was buoyed by honesty also. He shared the Commissioner's letter with the staff; nobody could deny what would happen if they didn't pull together and lift the students at Kinney High. Colby promised that when they did exceed state standards, he would personally drive to the Commissioner's office and deliver the letter back to him with a thank-you card from the staff. The intent to deliver a thank-you card seemed odd to the staff. Colby explained, "All motivation is good motivation. And,"—Colby smiled—"I want to make sure he takes Kinney High School off his mailing list."

Although the principals were anxious about how the teachers would respond to higher individual expectations, as it turned out, Grandpa Owen's belief that "Things are never as bad as you expect them to be" held true. Almost all the teachers responded to the personal accountability well; the care and coaching shown over the last two years gave them the trust necessary to show openness to feedback.

Unfortunately, *almost* was not *all*. A frustrated social studies teacher sat across the desk from Colby in his office.

"Frankly, I've had enough of this "lifting," or whatever you call it," Mr. Harrison said with his arms crossed. Colby had developed standards for Mr. Harrison based on the previous year's data, just as he had for the other teachers at Kinney High. Even though Mr. Harrison had been at the school for many years, the attendance for his classes was poor, and his failure rate was one of the highest on campus. By October, not much had improved.

As Colby looked at Mr. Harrison, he felt some sadness. Mr. Harrison was capable of good things, but he didn't seem to see his own talents, even though Colby had tried very hard to point them out. For whatever reason, Mr. Harrison had hardened his position, which stood in direct opposition to the standard Colby held for him.

Mr. Harrison's choices were leaving Colby no choice.

"Mr. Harrison, our students need and deserve teachers who have the courage to lift them to be their best selves. By the same token, our teachers need and deserve principals who have that courage. I'm not doing my job if I don't challenge you to be better."

Mr. Harrison glared at Colby. "You know," he said through clenched teeth, "you are awful young to be telling me, a veteran educator, anything about what good teaching looks like. Maybe you should focus a little more on reigning these kids and parents in, and less on cheerleading." He sneered as he said the last few words.

Colby was hurt and angered, but he took a deep breath and remembered to be honest and kind.

"Yes sir, you are right. I still have a lot to learn. As much as I have to learn, I do know a few things. I know I have tried very hard to help you grow, and I also know every choice we make has consequences. You have chosen to refuse coaching. Further, you have chosen not to grow as directed."

Colby took a deep breath. "Starting next Monday, you will be our new in-school suspension teacher. Your classroom management skills will be useful in your new role. I expect you to be successful in your new assignment."

Mr. Harrison stood up and walked out of Colby's office without a word, slamming the door behind him.

Colby closed his eyes and shook his head. Grandpa Owen was right. Leadership was costly sometimes.

One late June morning, a light rain fell as Colby rode the highway to the state capitol. He was keeping a promise; he had with him the warning letter he had received from the Commissioner of Education a little less than a year ago and a thank-you card signed by every staff member and teacher at Kinney High School. Dr. Yates and the school board members had also joined the fun, adding their names to the card. Colby had said over and over that the Commissioner should be thanked for providing the urgency to change. After staff development in August, Colby had framed the letter and hung it in a prominent place in the hallway so that staff and students could be reminded of the real consequences waiting if they couldn't pull together to lift Kinney High School.

With the cruise control set, Colby settled in for the two-hour journey. He had looked forward to this trip ever since the scores had come in a month ago. Dr. Yates hadn't called him to disclose the test results this time; instead, she had surprised him at his office. While planning for high school graduation, Colby, Brenden, and Amanda were shocked to see Dr. Yates walk in, tears streaming down her normally stoic and reserved face. She had endured the last three years right beside Colby, supporting and encouraging him on the good and bad days. Her joy that day was something Colby would always remember.

Truth be told, Colby wasn't incredibly surprised by the results from the state. Positive benchmark testing results, improved attendance, and improved student behavior indicated that the end-of-year results would be positive. Most teachers had responded brilliantly to the personal expectations and goals set at the beginning of the year. Colby, Brenden, and Amanda saw the teachers they were assigned to get better every six weeks.

As the teachers had become proficient in and then shown mastery of the attendance, behavior, and academic intervention systems, the student had followed suit with strong results of their own. Grandpa Owen's words, that Colby would feel his best as a leader when his caring, coaching, and courage helped his employees be and feel successful, rang true, and he smiled as he thought about his two grandpas' influence on him.

Colby thought through the events of the last three years, and the images flipped by like a movie picture reel. The fishing trip with Grandpa Wright, the day at the grocery store with Grandpa Owen, and the rocking chair and the day he learned to lift all ricocheted through his memory. He thought of Dr. Yates, Mr. Harrison, Brenden, Amanda, and all the high school teachers who had given everything they had to get Kinney High out of trouble with the state.

He reflected on learning how to show his care, and what that had meant for his relationships with his staff. He remembered Grandpa Owen coaching up his crew of sackers, and how he worked every day to win. He remembered the day he sat in a rocking chair and made the decision to leave his comfort zone and become a lifting leader. He remembered the courage it had taken to expect more from himself, his assistant principals, and his teachers.

He had lifted and been lifted. His grandpas had shown him how to be a lifting leader by the way they had raised him. Grandpa Owen considered the word "potential" to be a dirty word. "Colby," he said, "that just means you haven't realized the gifts you already have." His grandpas pushed him when they could easily have let him take the easy way out.

Those two guys had lifted him in their own unique ways, and as he traveled down the highway to see the Commissioner, Colby resolved to lift others as they did. He would pay what his grandpas had done for him forward; it was the least he could do.

Chapter 12

The Obstacles to Having Courage and the Consequences of Not Having Courage

The Third "C" to Lift: Courage

Courage separates the "good feelings" of support from the progress of lifting. When Colby understood what lifting leadership means, he understood the rocking chair metaphor. The rocking chair was comfortable and kept him from falling, but it did nothing to elevate him to a higher place until his grandpas had the courage to step forward and elevate his experience. To be great, we have to leave areas of comfort, and lifting leaders push us to do so.

The third "C" is the element of lifting that leaders sometimes struggle with the most. How much potential (Grandpa Owen called potential "wasted gifts") is unrealized because of lesser leaders and their lack of courage? How many millions of dollars are forfeited? How many lost souls remain lost? How many students never achieve the success owed to them? How many children become irresponsible adults because their parents lacked the courage to hold them accountable?

Regret is one thing lifting leaders commit to avoiding. When lifting leaders lay their heads down at night, they do so knowing they invested everything they had to help their employees be their best.

Courage is tough for one who wants to lift for two reasons: first, the right to lift must be earned, and second, it takes guts! Colby earned the right to lift Mr. Harrison: he cared and coached until he was blue in the face. Mr. Harrison's bad choices left Colby with only one good choice, which was to reassign him. Even though Colby knew it was the right thing to do, giving up on an employee hurts; but as Waldo Waldman says in his book *Never Fly Solo,* "there comes a time when quitting is the right answer." Colby's actions took courage, and that's what sets lifting leaders apart from lesser leaders.

Obstacles to Courage

The greatest obstacle to courage is fear. Fear of damaging employee relationships that leaders have worked hard to cultivate. Fear of hurting the feelings of employees whom leaders have come to like and respect. Fear of the politics that may come with holding an influential employee accountable. Fear of what other leaders may think. Fear of losing the position.

Fear is a part of leadership, and while that is an inescapable fact, knowing that what you are going through as a leader isn't rare or uncommon is comforting. It is part of the job. Leaders who wish to lift must accept that doing the hard things, such as holding employees accountable, is best for the organization and validates their right to lead.

My dad worked in the telephone business as an installer, and one of the unfortunate aspects of the job was cutting off service to customers who were in arrears. My dad often had to go on the customer's property to disconnect service. Sometimes, customers grew angry at my dad for what he was doing, but he always replied, "If I don't do this, the phone company will hire someone who will." That is really what it gets down to. Leadership requires courage, and those who lack courage generally don't get to keep leading.

By being a lifting leader, though, you accept the responsibility that comes with the choice to lift. You have cared for and coached your employees. By lifting, you have eliminated every excuse employees may have for underperforming. You were clear about the expectations you had, and the goals you set were fair and realistic. The employees were fully aware of how much they needed to grow. Surprised people get upset, but if you have done all the things a lifting leader should do, those courageous conversations that are necessary will generally be over before they start. In fact, lifting leaders more readily find the courage needed to hold an underperforming employee accountable than lesser leaders who haven't done the work caring and coaching.

Lifting means focusing on what is best for the employees in your organization. Servant leaders find ways to serve others, not themselves. Many leaders are constantly on the prowl for the next job and the opportunities that can be leveraged because of their positions. They network, they schmooze, they say nice things about other leaders, always with the intent of benefitting themselves. When lifting leaders come along who are committed to lifting their organization, they may be viewed as odd or as outsiders. No matter. Greatness is often misunderstood. Lifting leaders live lives of influence and understand the value of what they do. They believe in the "long game" and that nothing is free or easy. They don't play the favors game because they have no need to; results speak a lot louder than the whispers of those that don't understand or don't want to do the work excellence requires.

Finally, the fear of reprisal from holding influential employees accountable and the fear of losing a leadership position shouldn't interfere with leaders' ability to lift. Practicing lifting leadership means making the choice to serve employees and help them be their best. The success of the organization depends on this venture, and lifting leaders do it better than anyone. As a result, lifting leaders often have to deal with the opposite problem—the interest of other organizations in their success. The decision great leaders have to make is whether to go or stay.

Lesser leaders focus on "keeping a job" while lifting leaders focus on "doing the job." Lifting leaders do not allow what others might do blur or distort their image of what excellence looks like or diminish their interest in getting there. Results speak louder than the naysayers can. Keep lifting.

Consequences of Not Having Courage

Leaders must act with courage if they want to elevate the performance of their employees. Not acting with courage is a choice for which there are, of course, consequences.

Lesser leaders who don't act with courage accept they will never be the leaders they might have become. Not acting with courage ensures lesser leaders will never know what progress they could have led or the influence they could have had on the people and organizations they were affiliated with. By not holding people accountable, lesser leaders also put a limit on the level of success that organizations and the people in them can experience.

When leaders don't act with courage, instead neglecting to challenge their people to be better, they effectively abdicate their right to say they want what is best for their people. Winning is what defines success, and leaders lift when their people feel that success. Conversely, leaders fail when their people fail.

To recap, deciding not to act with courage entails the following:

- Accepting that you are a "lesser leader."
- Accepting that employees will never be their best.
- Accepting that the organization will never be its best.
- Accepting that for future opportunities, you will have to rely on others for help.
- Accepting that another leader could take your place.

Can you really accept the consequences of not having courage?

Lifting Leaders Need to Elevate Their Courage

Leaders who want to act with courage should consider the following questions:

- Have you earned the right to act with courage because of your care and coaching?
- Can your people honestly say they did not know your expectations or how to meet them?
- Are the standards and goals you set for your employees ambiguous in any way?
- Were those standards and goals fair and reasonable?
- Did you continue to care and coach throughout the process of lifting?
- Was your door open for questions and communication throughout the process of lifting?
- Are employees making bad choices, or are uncontrollable factors hindering their performance?
- How will you feel when your organization doesn't elevate because of your fear of doing the right thing?
- If you've done all you can do to care and coach, what are you waiting on before having that courageous conversation?

One Last Thing About Courage

You were appointed the leader. You are the principal. Here is your shot to do something that will change your life and the lives of the people lucky enough to know you. You've put the work in caring and coaching. You are invested. Nobody has earned the right to lift as you have. Be courageous and elevate those who look to you for guidance, strength, and wisdom! Everything rises and falls on leadership; will you help your people rise? Will you lift?

PART
IV

A WAY TO LIFT

Chapter 13

Lift: A Way

As ideas evolve, they inevitably face the question of application: How do we make use of this idea in a way that will be beneficial now? This question is immensely important. Until an idea grows legs and becomes something practical, it is of little value to us.

This chapter gives you, the school leader, a way to apply the lifting tenets. When we lift, we invest in the growth of others. We commit to bringing out the greatness we see in our teachers. As lifting leaders, we recognize that the power of any organization comes from the aptitude and effort of its people.

This section provides a game plan that marries the lifting formula to a time-tested, research-based form of developmental supervision derived from the work of distinguished author and professor Carl Glickman. The process discussed in this section will:

- Provide you with a model that evaluates the past performance of teachers based on their will and skill.
- Provide you the ability to situationally apply the lifting formula.

- Provide you with a way to evaluate your own leadership skill in lifting teachers to be their best.

A brief description of Carl Glickman's work is a necessary preface to the development of a greater understanding of how principals might practice the art of lifting on their campus. From there, the lifting formula shows how leaders can identify whether coaching or courage is required to elevate teachers to excellence.

My current role as a district educational leader allows me to practice this process with campus administrators. The conversations this process elicits, and the questions it creates, help develop the focus needed to produce professional development plans for all teachers. All teachers can always improve, which is precisely what our present and future students are counting on.

Glickman Model

Carl Glickman is known for his work in education, especially in the field of developmental supervision. Of the many books he has written, the one I have leaned on over the years is *Leadership for Learning: How to Help Teachers Succeed* (2002). Any school leader wanting to learn more about how to improve classroom teaching and learning should pick up this book.

Glickman's book is technical and prescriptive, but it uses a situational approach in discussing ways to help teachers improve. What follows is a simplified version of what the Glickman

Model is and how I teach it to principals. For the purpose of simplification, I take some liberty with the terms used in the following description. Anyone comparing what Dr. Glickman brought to developmental supervision with what I provide in this book will see stark similarities and minor differences.

The variables we will use in the Glickman Model are "will" and "skill." Will designates effort and involves the choices our teachers make for students. Will encompasses a variety of things germane to fulfilling the duties of being a teacher. Examples include:

- Being on time.
- Being positive.
- Meeting deadlines.
- Having a growth mindset.
- Investing in and caring for students and co-workers.

Scoring high marks in the above categories takes little talent, but the choices made regarding these things greatly affect the level of success one can attain.

Skill, as you can probably guess, is the ability teachers have to ply their trade. Skill is most closely aligned with attributes that are learned, either through teacher preparation courses or through the greatest teacher, experience. Teaching skills include:

- Knowledge and successful application of classroom management.
- Knowledge and successful application of curriculum.

- Knowledge and successful application of engaging instruction.
- Knowledge and successful application of assessment.
- Knowledge and successful application of student interventions.

Whereas "will" is choice-driven, "skill" is a learned attribute that some teachers have and some do not.

The question that inevitably comes up when I work with principals is this: "Can the decision not to practice a skill I know a teacher has be considered an effort issue?" I always respond, "How do you know they have that skill?" Before we call it an effort issue, we must know for certain teachers have been coached on that particular skill. We must never assume that teachers know or don't know. The right to lift is earned, and caring and coaching should always come before any perception of a lack of will in areas of skill.

Below is the adapted "lifting" version of Dr. Glickman's model:

Quad 3 (Low Will, High Skill)	**Quad 4** (High Will, High Skill)
Quad 2 (High Will, Low Skill)	**Quad 1** (Low Will, Low Skill)

The basic idea is that every teacher falls into one of these quadrants. When school leaders see this model for the first time, they tend to over-complicate and over-think where teachers fall within it, which led me to create the following "rules of engagement." First, skill can be coached, will cannot. Anyone with a working level of abstraction can learn and apply the skills that contribute to teaching well. Lack of will, on the other hand, is a heart issue that can only be resolved by the owner. Second, teachers are the number one reason why students succeed or fail. This crucial reminder emphasizes the importance of spending time on an activity like this. Third, going with the gut when considering where teachers fall in the quadrants is okay. While numbers always help justify a line of thinking and certainly help in goal-setting, the purpose of this activity is not to obtain perfect accuracy, but to start a conversation about how to train teachers to be their best.

Before we delve into what this training looks like for principals, let's discuss the different quadrants and what kinds of teachers fall into each one.

Quad 1: Low Will, Low Skill

Teachers in this quadrant need to grow or go. The sad fact is that not everyone with a certificate to teach should be a teacher, just as not everyone with a medical degree or a law degree should be a doctor or lawyer. Dr. Glickman calls these educators "teacher dropouts" (Glickman, 2002, p. 87) because they "go through the minimal motions in order to keep a job" and "they have little motivation for improving their competencies" (Glickman, 2002, p. 87). Teachers in this category do a disservice to the students at the schools they work in, and principals that allow these teachers to persist in their roles bear a great deal of the fault.

Quad 2: High Will, Low Skill

Teachers in this category are often brand new to the profession and have not had the time or coaching needed to develop their skills. It is imperative that school leaders identify who these "unfocused workers" (Glickman, 2002, p. 89) are before they burn out from energy expended on unproductive causes in the classroom. The advantage Quad 2 teachers have is that they are often coachable, and with the right principal they can become good teachers over time.

Quad 3: Low Will, High Skill

The teachers in this quadrant are full of potential but make the choice to be less than what they could be for students. Dr. Glickman calls this group "analytical observers" (Glickman, 2002, p. 89). Generally, these teachers have a lot of experience but have lost their fire for the promise of education and just go through the day. Unfortunately, sometimes they stay at the same school for many years and develop a great deal of influence, thwarting progress that would be great for students but would overthrow what they have become accustomed to. These teachers must be forced to decide to either pursue excellence and realize their Quad 4 potential or find another school that will allow them to remain stagnant. Principals who lift cannot allow Quad 3 teachers to remain Quad 3 teachers at their schools.

Quad 4: High Will, High Skill

These are the rock star teachers principals yearn for and students need. They show up early and stay late. They take on any task delegated to them and always look for ways to improve, although they already have the best scores in the county. Dr. Glickman calls this group "professionals," and I can think of no better term. Professionals do their jobs even when they don't feel like it, and while Quad 4 teachers may not always be 100%, they give you 100% of what they have on any given day. I always tell principals during my training that if they can ever get their campus to a place where there are only Quad 4s in the classrooms, their coming to work as the principal becomes optional. They won't have student issues because students won't want to leave the learning happening in classrooms. They won't have teacher issues because Quad 4s are too immersed in their work to have time to cause problems with other teachers. They won't have parent issues because Quad 4s do not have parent issues. Finally, they won't have superintendent problems because the test scores will be above reproach and the budget will always be balanced, since Quad 4s aren't in it for the money. Quad 4s work because they want to make a difference in students' lives.

After hearing that description, principals find it fairly easy to place teachers in different quadrants. They bring their campus teacher lists (the activity can be done for paraprofessionals and other staff members as well) and they put initials in the quadrants where they think the teachers belong. It ends up looking something like this:

IA OB		VN CT	
SW RA	**Q3**	WR GG	**Q4**
SM		EO	
AG HH		HN	
KW TV	**Q2**	BR	**Q1**
SS			

As principals put initials in each category, the best question in the universe (why?) comes up frequently. Engaging this question reveals how strong a case the principals can make for their decisions. Such reflection is the beginning of what ultimately becomes a professional development plan for each teacher, with the goal being to grow as many faculty members into Quad 4s as possible. For those who lack the will to fulfill their potential, the principals' challenge is to minimize or remove the influence their bad choices have on the schools' students. I always remind principals that teachers get paid; students do not.

Application of Lift

Now that principals have a method for categorizing teachers' levels of efficacy, the question arises, "How do we grow them?" Lifting leaders follow the three Cs by showing care to all teachers, coaching Quad 2s, and having courageous conversations with Quad 3s.

Caring for All

Caring for teachers is the first priority for principals interested in seeing them become their best. As Colby learned, teachers will give a lot more to leaders they feel are committed to them, the school, and the students.

Depicted visually, caring looks like this:

CARE					
IA OB SW RA SM	**Q3**		VN CT WR GG EO	**Q4**	
AG HH KW TV SS	**Q2**		HN BR	**Q1**	
CARE					

All teachers, regardless of which quadrant they inhabit, need to know you, their leader, care about them. People aren't made equal, so why should teachers be any different? Some teachers will have a longer way to go, just as some principals have a longer way to go. As leaders, we have to earn the right to lift, and we earn that right by genuinely caring for our teachers.

Coaching Quad 2 Teachers

Everyone needs a coach, some more than others. Quad 2 teachers have the will but lack the skill needed to become Quad 4s. Quad 2 teachers work hard, but often on the wrong things. They scurry around, trying this or that, and they feel discouraged when the results don't line up with their effort. Absentee principals, who expect teachers to figure things out on their own, play a large part in why most teachers leave the field of education within five years. With no one to lean on for guidance, Quad 2 teachers eventually either leave the classroom or become Quad 1 teachers. Campus leaders must know their campus and teacher data well enough to make good decisions on how best to coach their Quad 2s before it is too late. To visualize:

IA	OB		VN	CT	
SW	RA	**Q3**	WR	GG	**Q4**
SM			EO		
AG	HH		HN		
KW	TV	**Q2**	BR		**Q1**
SS					

The best time to coach is when people want the coaching. Quad 2s are often the most fun to work with because they listen to and at least try to apply the ideas of the campus leader. Remember that teachers always listen better and work harder for principals they believe care about them. The right to lift is earned.

Having Courage with Quad 3s

Quad 3 teachers weren't always Quad 3 teachers. Because they have impressive skills, they obviously put the work in at some point. Most of the time, Quad 3 teachers are veteran teachers who lost the rookie mindset needed to continue growing as educators. This happens for myriad reasons. Sometimes life issues outside of school drain their passion. Also, some teachers are more open to change than others. Education is nothing but change, so those that resist it can fall into this category. Sometimes conflicts with team members or campus leadership can impact the will Quad 3 teachers have to make good decisions for students.

Regardless of the reasons Quad 3 teachers are Quad 3 teachers, they cannot remain Quad 3 teachers. Quad 3 teachers have the potential to be great, and their students need them to be. Quad 3 teachers can move right in the Glickman Model and become Quad 4 teachers or move left and leave the organization. Lifting leaders are committed to helping teachers be their best, and they understand that doing so involves having courageous conversations at times. To visualize:

IA OB SW RA **Q3** SM	VN CT WR GG **Q4** EO	
AG HH KW TV **Q2** SS	HN BR **Q1**	

Before any courageous conversations happen, leaders must remember that the right to lift is earned. Have they shown enough care? Have they done enough coaching to know the Quad 3 teacher has the skills necessary to carry out the objective? Have they thoroughly communicated the expectations for conducting business on the school campus?

Ultimately, lifting leaders must eliminate any and all excuses for why Quad 3 teachers choose to be Quad 3 teachers. Once it is clear the teachers are choosing to be less than their best, lifting leaders must address the issue and create plans for future success. Quad 3 teachers will generally either grow or go when confronted. Sometimes, despite receiving great care and coaching, Quad 3 teachers go underground and use their influence to circumvent or sabotage lifting leaders. Don't let this possibility deter you or derail your focus on doing what is best for the kids! True lifting leaders keep their eyes on their purpose and sleep well at night, knowing they have done all they can each day to help teachers be their best for the students they teach.

A Word about Quad 4 Teachers

Quad 4 teachers are awesome teachers who exhibit the skill and will each day to influence students in positive ways. They are committed professionals who do the right thing when no one is looking. As a principal, you cherish these teachers. A lifting leader should know two things about Quad 4 teachers:

- Quad 4 teachers can still grow.
- Quad 4 teachers can become Quad 3 teachers.

We can all get better, and Quad 4 teachers are no different. Within Quad 4, we can place teachers where they are in comparison to their Quad 4 colleagues. The quality and quantity of data at principals' disposal determines the precision of this exercise. To visualize:

IA	OB		VN	CT →	
SW	RA	**Q3**	WR →	GG →	**Q4**
SM			EO →		
AG	HH		HN		
KW	TV	**Q2**	BR		**Q1**
SS					

Whereas Quad 1, Quad 2 and Quad 3 teachers' improvement is somewhat directed by the lifting leader, Quad 4s have earned the right to own their growth. Quad 4 teachers become the best because they have a growth mindset, so they naturally lean into positive change instead of running from it. The best thing lifting leaders can do with Quad 4 teachers is provide an environment of high expectations and a culture of excellence. Quad 4s thrive in such conditions.

Lifting leaders' primary responsibility regarding Quad 4 teachers is keeping them Quad 4 teachers. Quad 4 teachers can slide into Quad 3—the last thing any leader needs. Why would Quad 4s regress? If you want the reasons, consider why Quad 3s are Quad 3s. Many of a campus's Quad 3 teachers were likely Quad 4s at some point!

To keep Quad 4 teachers happy, leaders must care enough about them to know what moves them. Some teachers appreciate recognition for their excellence, and others run from praise. Most—if not all—principals who lift were Quad 4 teachers at some point, so some Quad 4s have aspirations of becoming campus leaders themselves. Help them be what they want to be! Investing in the growth of the very best teachers you have is a sure way to keep them on your campus until it is time for them to become lifting leaders themselves.

Parting Words

There really is nothing better for a principal who lifts than seeing teachers fulfill their potential until they become professionals. Lifting leaders feel a quiet pride when their teachers take the steps necessary to become their best. Teachers are the primary influencers of student success—when teachers get better, so do students.

I leave you with a call to action: as a principal, be your best. Show your care, coach with enthusiasm, and be bold when courage is needed. Lift!

References

Fullan, M. (2009). Large-scale reform comes of age. *Journal of Educational Change*, 10(2), 101-113. doi:10.1007/s10833-009-9108-z

Glickman, C. D. (2002). *Leadership for Learning*, Alexandria, VA: ASCD.

Holiday, R. (2014). *The Obstacle is the Way*. New York, NY. Penguin Group.

U.S. Senate. (1977). *Committee Report on Educational Opportunity*. p. 56.

Acknowledgments

I am grateful to many people involved in this book's creation and development. Thanks to Brown Books and all the fine people who helped me shape this project into its final form. Specifically, thanks to Milli Brown for agreeing to partner with me and to Bonnie Hearn Hill for her amazing work shaping the initial manuscript into something I am proud of. I have learned a great deal about the publishing process in the last few months, and I've enjoyed the experience for the most part.

I am grateful to my friends David Flowers and Allen Pack for their constant support and feedback. It took a few years to get to this point, and they have been with me for the duration. This book wouldn't have made it to print without their timely advice and encouragement. They lifted me multiple times during the process, and I am lucky they are part of my circle.

I am grateful to my wife Amanda for her support and her skill in editing and revising my earliest drafts. I'm not sure I would have been taken seriously as an author had she not refined my rough scribblings into something sensible to people other than me.

As Allen and I have discussed, we don't really know the influence this book will have; how do authors ever really know? For those that bought this book, I am grateful to each of you for giving it a chance to inform and elevate your practice. I know how hard being a principal is, but the work is worth doing, and the world needs you to be great at it. I hope this book lifts you.

About the Author

For over twenty-two years, Walter Peddy has served in public education as a teacher, coach, campus administrator, district administrator, and district superintendent. He has written several articles for leadership journals while also completing his doctorate of educational leadership at Stephen F. Austin State University in Nacogdoches, Texas. He has also presented at state and national conventions on various school leadership topics. He is currently the assistant superintendent of curriculum and instruction at Huntington ISD. When time permits, he moonlights as a leadership trainer and consultant for district leadership teams in Texas and Louisiana. Visit www.leadingislifting.com to set up leadership training for your district leadership team.